Retirement Income Masters
Secrets of the Pros

By Tom Hegna

With Contributions By:
Dick Austin
Briggs Matsko
John H. Curry
John P. Schwan
John L. Olsen
Michael Gordon
John W. Homer
Curtis Cloke
Michael Kitces
Bob Hartman
Rao K. Garuda
Christie Mueller
Joseph W. Jordan
Dave Christy

Table of Contents

Preface..9

Acknowledgements...11

Introduction...15

Part 1: Planning...17

    Chapter 1: Retirement Is a New Dawn.........................19

    Briggs Matsko, CFP®, CRPC® / Lincoln Financial Advisors / Retirement Security Centers

    Chapter 2: The Secure Retirement Method.................31

    John H. Curry, CLU®, ChFC®, AEP®, MSFS, CLTC / North Florida Financial Corporation

    Chapter 3: The Ideal Plan Process..............................45

    John P. Schwan / Schwan Financial Group

Part 2: Strategies..59

    Chapter 4: An Annuity Is Not an Investment, It's an Income Stream..61

    John L. Olsen, CLU®, ChFC®, AEP® / Olsen Financial Group

    Chapter 5: Income Annuities in the Context of Holistic Retirement Management.............................71

    Michael Gordon / Longbridge Investments

    Chapter 6: Cinderella Slipper Strategies....................79

    John W. Homer, CLU® / Oxford Financial Group

Part 3: Solutions...95

    Chapter 7: Separating the Truth from the Bull...........97

Curtis Cloke, CLTC, LUTCF / Acuity Financial / Thrive Income Distribution System®

Chapter 8: Ensuring Safe Withdrawal Rates Aren't "Too Risky" nor "Too Safe"...........................**115**

Michael Kitces, MSFS, MTAX, CFP®, CLU®, ChFC®, RHU®, REBC®, CASL® / Pinnacle Advisory Group / The Kitces Report

Chapter 9: Solutions for the Uncertainty of Retirement Income Needs...........................**127**

Richard P. Austin, CLU®, ChFC®, CRC®, Consultant to the Financial Services Industry

Chapter 10: Designing the Ideal Income Solution....**141**

Bob Hartman, CLU®, ChFC®, CASL® / New York Life

Part 4: The Role of the Advisor...........................**153**

Chapter 11: Retaining Clients is the Number One Key to Growth...........................**155**

Dave Christy / National Property & Casualty Agency

Chapter 12: It's Not About Fees—It's About Value and Performance...........................**165**

Christie Mueller / New York Life / Christie Mueller & Associates

Chapter 13: Significantly Influencing Clients' Lives....**175**

Joseph W. Jordan / Independent Consultant

Chapter 14: How Much of a Difference Can You Make?...........................**187**

Rao K. Garuda, CLU®, ChFC® / Associated Concepts Agency / First Financial Resources

Conclusion...........................**199**

Preface

"The first person to live to 150 is alive today."

The first time that I saw Prudential's billboard, I almost drove off the road. I was entering a tunnel in New York City and I mulled that sentence over and over the entire ride underground. When I reemerged, I was blinded by the light.

Prudential's new campaign is a bold prediction.[1] Yet, people today are living longer than in the past. Advances in medical technology and treatment are lowering mortality rates and increasing life expectancies. While we may be thrilled to spend that much more time with our grandchildren and great-grandchildren, how is this affecting the way we spend our money? How do we financially plan for this great unknown? While we can never pinpoint the day we are going to die, we had previously been able to guess based on averages. But now, who knows what scientists are going to come up with next? Although we may not see the elixir of life any time soon, we do have to face the changing impacts that increased life expectancies place on our lives, and the lives of our clients.

As financial advisors, we must be the reassuring guide in our clients' lives, leading them toward sound decisions and avoiding potentially destructive ones. We have to quiet their greatest fear: the fear of outliving their money. In *Paychecks and Playchecks*, I challenged my readers to do their own due diligence: Research their financial advisors and search for indicators of professionalism, ethics, and excellence. I have written this second book as a follow-up—I have done my due diligence and have found some of the top Masters of Paychecks and Playchecks. Having traveled extensively

---

[1] For more information about Prudential's 2013 campaign, please visit http://news.prudential.com/article_display. cfm?article_id=6490.

over the United States, speaking to countless advisors and gaining new insight from their perspective, I have found myself surrounded by men and women who make a difference in their clients' lives. Included in the following chapters are industry leaders, Top of the Table agents, innovators, and thought leaders. While I could never include every great financial advisor whom I have met, I have selected a sample of the best of the best—the Masters, if you will. These are the men and women who should be modeled after and learned from, as I myself have done. Most importantly, these are the advisors who can best assuage their clients' worries about the future.

Thanks in large part to the overwhelmingly positive response to my first book, *Paychecks and Playchecks*, I have set out, once again, to help make retirement planning less intimidating. I could never fully voice how grateful I am for the great response to my first book and how excited I am to embark on a new journey for you, the advisor. Without financial advisors, we would all be lost, unsure of how to proceed into our retirement years and beyond. I have learned from so many remarkable colleagues and mentors; their fresh and experienced perspectives have been invaluable. And I hope that with Retirement Income Masters: Secrets of the Pros, I will be able to impart my vision and perspective to you, along with the indispensable insight of the advisors whom I hold in the highest regard.

In *Paychecks and Playchecks*, I stressed the math and science behind my reasoning. In Retirement Income Masters, I am more focused on the emotional connection that makes the math and science viable. Through these incredible success stories, I aim to show advisors who may not have always had it easy, but who determinedly pushed on until it finally "clicked."

I hope that through these stories, it will click for you, too.

Acknowledgements

I would like to sincerely thank each of the people I focused on in this book. It was an incredible experience that I certainly will never forget. I must also thank Susan Wright and Andrea Weidknecht for their great work as well. Let me share with you the process we used to put this book together. I say "we" because I simply could not have put this book together without the help of Susan Wright, CLU®, ChFC®, RHU®, REBC®, CSA, CLTC, CCFC, CSS, ADPA®. With my near-daily criss-crossing of the country, there was just no way I could get this book done without some help. After reviewing 20–30 resumes of financial writers, my final interviews proved fruitful. Susan was the ideal candidate: not only does she have an extensive background in the financial services industry, but when I read her materials, I felt like I was reading my own writing. She writes clearly and simply—just as I try to do.

The process was a simple one: We interviewed every advisor together, recording the interviews, then Susan would write the first draft and send it to me. From there, I would add, delete, and change as I wanted. I personalized each chapter based on my personal knowledge of the person. I would then send my draft to the editor, Andrea Weidknecht, who would then restructure it into a standardized storyline and send it back to me. I would make additional edits and then forward it to the person we were highlighting to make sure that our chapter was accurate and clear.

The final steps are always the most challenging. A number of compliance departments got involved, reviewing the chapters of their advisors. I have worked extensively with many company compliance officers. We were able to work out any differences of opinion to create compelling yet compliant chapters. These steps certainly added a couple of months to the editing process.

Although the process seems like it might be a little clunky, it flowed smoother than I could have anticipated. Each step made the chapter better! I think Susan, Andrea, and I have to say this was an incredible experience.

Thank you to everyone at Acanthus Publishing who contributed to the success of this second book. I would like to especially acknowledge Paige Stover Hague, George Kasparian, Ian Nichols, Jacqueline de la Rosa, Hillary Rosander, Morgan Rosenberg, Stephanie Callan, and Robert Roussel for their expert assistance.

Finally, I want to again acknowledge each of the advisors who made this book possible. Each of the people we focused on was passionate about what they did. They all came at the retirement income problem from a different angle. Believe it or not, each comes out with a slightly different process and slightly different focus. Their solutions, however, are remarkably similar. And I think that is where you can benefit the most.

Introduction

This book is a book for advisors by advisors. It is for professional financial advisors who really want to work in the retirement income market. The ideas and stories contained here will put your head and shoulders above the average advisor.

Each of us has our own strengths and weaknesses. We should forever try to learn from others to improve our weaknesses, and share our strengths. For this reason, I have divided Retirement Income Masters into four parts: Planning, Strategies, Solutions, and The Role of the Advisor. For each section, I have pinpointed the advisors who truly "get" it. They know how to plan for their client's future; they are pros at coming up with strategies to solve for financial challenges; they can find solutions to any problem; and they understand what it means to be an advisor. They are the Masters.

The best advisors view planning for retirement as a process to create a future that is best for the client. By planning, clients can maintain financial independence, economic freedom, and their dignity. Of the advisors in this book, Briggs Matsko, John Curry, and John Schwan look to that plan as the ultimate guide. They know that creating a plan together with clients gives them the confidence needed to approach retirement.

The financial advisors who specialize in strategies know how to dig deep into the worries of clients and find a way to allay these anxieties. They are the advisors who understand how to position products and vehicles through models and questioning. I position John Olsen, Michael Gordon, and John Homer as these advisors. They understand risk and how to find ways to avoid it. And their clients receive specific advice based on their own perceptions of risk and retirement.

In these uncertain times, creativity is the only solution to answer clients' individual situations and problems. Richard Austin, Bob Hartman, Curtis Cloke, and Michael Kitces solve for the strongest combination of products to deliver the best outcome for clients. Through research into each client's situation, their results solve the risk.

While any financial advisor must know their role to be successful, it is the advisor who holds their responsibility in clients' lives as the most esteemed part of their job. They are the ones who truly know what it is to be an advisor. Dave Christy, Christie Mueller, Joe Jordan, and Rao Garuda are such advisors in this book. They know how important it is to gain trust by connecting emotionally before any advising relationship can start. Once that relationship is developed, they will create lasting clients who hold the potential of generations through this respect.

While every advisor I have mentioned is skillful in each of these four aspects of advising, I wanted to highlight the different facets that make up an advisor's job. By reading the advisor's stories and the expertise they have developed along the way, I hope that you will recognize your own strengths and weaknesses, and take the advice they are imparting.

So if you are a financial advisor who really wants to work in the retirement income market, let's get started!

Retirement Income Masters: Secrets of the Pros

PART ONE

PLANNING

Chapter 1: Retirement Is a New Dawn

"We like to think of ourselves in many ways as your 'walking reality check' because we don't take short cuts, we'd rather take the time necessary to demonstrate through in-depth analysis, visual representation, and face to face discussions about the road that currently lies ahead. With this as our baseline we can then map the best path forward together." [2]

Briggs Matsko, CFP®, CRPC®
Lincoln Financial Advisors / Retirement Security Centers

Briggs Matsko
(Photo courtesy of Briggs Matsko)

While clients may have abstract ideas of what they want their retirement to look like, they may be lost as to how to actually implement their ideas into action. This is where the job of a financial advisor comes into play. Only by listening, looking at the numbers, and drafting a strategic plan that the client understands can an advisor help turn a client's goals into a reality.

As a CERTIFIED FINANCIAL PLANNER™ practitioner, Briggs Matsko, CFP®, CRPC®, of Retirement Security Centers, believes in an objective, process-driven approach that considers not only quantitative data, but also client values, goals, and desires. His goal is to help people crystallize their vision of retirement from a psychological as well as a financial perspective.

By having an in-depth conversation with clients that involves asking specific questions, Briggs is able to obtain more meaningful information from clients and can therefore move forward with creating a customized plan that addresses their specific financial

2 "About Us," Retirement Security Centers™, 2013, http://www.retirementsecuritycenters.com/About-Us.1.htm.

needs and goals.[3]

> Briggs always valued the hard workers who made this country run. Growing up near Pittsburgh, Pennsylvania, he was the son of a World War II veteran who returned home to work in the steel mills. While attending Beaver County Community College and Penn State University, Briggs worked for a large shoe company that eventually transferred him to California, then to Kansas City. He later headed west again and settled in the Sacramento (CA) area.
>
> It was while he was living in Kansas City that Briggs was initially recommended by a neighbor to consider a career in financial services. So, still in his mid-20s, Briggs began working with Aetna; two years later, he moved to Lincoln Financial Advisors, where he focused on working with school teachers in the 403(b) market.
>
> He soon added hospitals and healthcare systems to his client focus. Over the next twenty years, he built his planning practice to include 25 planners and staff, servicing 33 healthcare institutions. Collectively they enrolled over 30,000 employees and now have close to $1 billion in client invested assets.

While Briggs now works with families and individuals of all ages, his passion lies in the area of retirement income distribution. As an income distribution specialist, he works closely with his clients to categorize expenses and link them to income sources. His most crucial objective is to ensure that clients do not run out of money for their core expenses in retirement. His mission is to help them maintain their financial independence, economic freedom, and dignity.

He and his team provide comprehensive, fee-based financial planning and other financial services to individuals and institutional clients, which include some of the nation's largest healthcare systems.

3 "Briggs Matsko, CFP®, CRPC®," Retirement Security Centers™, 2013, http://www.retirementsecuritycenters. com/ecard.cfm?ID=487056.

By the early 1990s, Briggs began to realize that there weren't many planners working in the income distribution market. He could see the potential in this niche, having annuitized his first fixed annuity contract in the 1980s—a contract whose beneficiary is still alive today and benefitting from the funds.

Through speaking engagements, interviews with the media, demographic research, and 30 years of client experience, Briggs Matsko, CFP®, CRPC® is recognized nationally for his work on retirement income distribution. He shares that knowledge with others by educating financial professionals nationwide about his unique processes.

E.A.S.E. Process

[Source: © Retirement Security Centers, 2013]

He is a firm believer in using a defined, understandable, and succinct process with clients. This four-step method, called the EASE Process, includes the following conversations with clients:

- **"Step 1 – Envision":** The first step entails getting a deeper understanding of what clients' issues are, both currently and for retirement. Once Briggs understands where a client wants to go in terms of their vision and goals, he and his team separate out the goals that relate to Core, Joy, and Legacy expenses, and subsequently match these expenses to the client's income and assets.

- **"Step 2 – Analyze":** Once the client's information has been separated into the appropriate goal categories, Briggs and his team further analyze it using their technology and, in turn, help the client to literally "see" a vision of their retirement lifestyle.

- **"Step 3 – Solutions":** In the third step of the EASE Process, Briggs and his team sit down with their clients in order to go over the recommended financial solutions and strategies. Prior to moving forward on any strategy, though, they make sure that all of the clients'—and their families'—questions are answered.

- **"Step 4 – Evaluate":** No matter how good a financial plan is, it should be reviewed on a regular basis in order to account for any changes in a client's life, such as a change in health status, birth or death of a family member, and other scenarios. It is at this time that any required changes to the financial plan will be implemented.[4]

Because financial planning is truly an ongoing process, using the EASE Process works to ensure that plans are able to evolve into goals for the future. This method leaves room for any type of change or plan alteration that may need to be incorporated along the way.

In conjunction with the EASE Process, Briggs and his team also use a Retirement Income Matrix with their clients. This three-level, pyramid-shaped diagram helps clients to further envision how they

---

4 "The-Ease Process," Retirement Security Centers™, 2013, http://www.retirementsecuritycenters.com/The-EASE-Process.9.htm.

will transfer their goals and dreams using actual asset and income strategies.

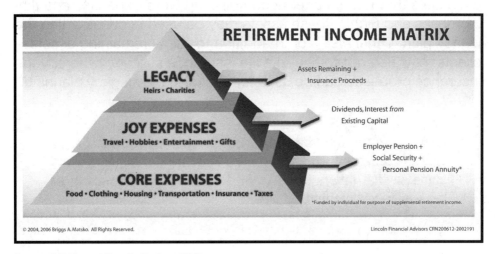

RETIREMENT INCOME MATRIX

LEGACY
Heirs • Charities

JOY EXPENSES
Travel • Hobbies • Entertainment • Gifts

CORE EXPENSES
Food • Clothing • Housing • Transportation • Insurance • Taxes

Assets Remaining +
Insurance Proceeds

Dividends, Interest *from*
Existing Capital

Employer Pension +
Social Security +
Personal Pension Annuity*

*Funded by individual for purpose of supplemental retirement income.

© 2004, 2006 Briggs A. Matsko. All Rights Reserved.   Lincoln Financial Advisors CRN200612-2002191

Source: © Retirement Security Centers, 2013]

The bottom level, Core Expenses, makes up the foundation of the pyramid. The bulk of the income in this level will typically come from Social Security, employer pensions if applicable, and annuity income strategies. Clients use these designated income streams to take care of their basic living expenses, such as food, clothing, housing, and other regular costs, like taxes and insurance. Once these basic living expenses are accounted for, clients have much more leeway in what they do with the remainder of their assets.[5]

The middle level of the pyramid combines Joy Expenses and Goals. These large financial aspirations may include amassing college savings for a child or grandchild, purchasing a boat or RV, or leasing or buying a vacation home. The income for these expenditures is generally derived—or remaining—from dividends and interest coming out of the clients' existing capital. Because the clients have already secured the income for ongoing daily costs, the income for this second level can be spent much more worry-free on things that many may consider to be "wants" versus "needs." [6]

5 Brian Hall, "Putting Boomers in the Driver's Seat: A Process-Driven Approach Is Key to Matsko's Success with Income Distribution for Baby Boomers," Round the Table, January/February 2008, http://www.gibbs-soell.com/wp-content/uploads/2010/02/Putting_Boomers_in_the_Drivers_Seat_Feb_2008.pdf.
6 Ibid.

The top of the pyramid represents Legacy, something clients may wish to leave for their heirs or to charitable organizations. If there are assets that remain after accomplishing Core Expenses and Joy Expenses and Goals, these assets may be used in constructing the legacy plan. Otherwise—or in addition to these remaining assets—clients may also opt to set up a life insurance strategy, whereby the insurance proceeds can be used for capital in their legacy planning.[7]

> **Upon going through the Retirement Income Matrix, one couple was so impressed with the process that they developed a board game so that others could walk through the techniques in an easy-to-follow manner.**

Case Study

Sometimes visualizing what they currently have versus what they want will ease clients' unrealistic retirement expectations. Briggs recalls a couple from California who had dreams of a retirement that included very high expenses.

After running an analysis, Briggs demonstrated how their particular goal was not possible. He was even able to pinpoint, given certain assumptions, exactly when the couple would run out of money if they pursued that particular retirement lifestyle.

Although this wasn't what the clients wanted to hear, the visual analysis did prove to the clients that they would run into financial trouble in the near future. Consequently, by understanding longevity, expense, and rate of return risk, Briggs was able to help them put together a financial strategy that was more realistic over the long term based on their situation.

In addition to the EASE process and the Retirement Income Matrix, Briggs and his partner, Jeff Maas, CFP®, ChFC®, CRPC®,

---

7 Brian Hall, "Putting Boomers in the Driver's Seat."

have co-founded Retirement Security Centers (RSC). Aware that millions of baby boomers are in the midst of entering or approaching retirement, they created RSC to provide them with a resource where they could get objective, process-driven, fee-based advice without feeling pressured to buy a product.

RSC offers clients the ability to work with a professional advisor using "what-if" scenarios, where the client is truly in the driver's seat through the use of interactive technology. Presentations can also be done using web conference technology.

Briggs and Jeff envisioned RSC as serving middle America—a currently underserved market in the area of retirement planning. While those with high net worth have access to many advisors, Briggs and Jeff wanted to give the mass affluent (who might not be inclined to seek out professional advice) a place to get objective guidance through a process.

With RSC, they know that retirees and those approaching retirement will be able to connect on a financial and emotional level. Retirement isn't just about having enough income; it's about being able to live the goals that you've been planning for all along. For this reason, they penned the Retirement Security Center Doctrine.[8]

---

8 "Our Values," Retirement Security Centers™, June 2013, http://www.retirementsecuritycenters.com/Our-Values.6.htm.

THE RSC DOCTRINE

RETIREMENT SECURITY CENTERS
DEFINE YOUR FUTURE

RETIREMENT IS A NEW DAWN.

EMBRACE THE GRAY. CONTINUE TO WRITE YOUR STORY. STAY ENGAGED. LIVE YOUR LIFE TO THE FULLEST. YOU ARE THE MASTER OF YOUR CALENDAR. **DREAM YOUR NEXT ADVENTURE.** GET UP EARLY, GET UP LATE, WATCH YOUR FAVORITE MOVIE MORE THAN ONCE. ENJOY A SUNRISE AND A SUNSET IN THE SAME DAY.

EXPLORE NEW HORIZONS. TRAVEL FAR AND WIDE. NURTURE YOUR INTERESTS AND FOLLOW YOUR PASSIONS. PURSUE THE HOBBY YOU ALWAYS SAID YOU WOULD. IT IS NEVER TOO LATE TO TRY.

INSTEAD OF JUMPING **EASE INTO RETIREMENT.** EXPLORE YOUR POSSIBILITIES.

ENJOY THE NEW DEFINITION OF NORMAL IN YOUR LIFE. BE A MENTOR, A COACH, AN INSPIRATION. SHARE YOUR WISDOM AND EXPERIENCES. MAKE A DIFFERENCE IN THE WORLD. RENEW OLD FRIENDSHIPS AND DEVELOP NEW ONES. COUNT YOUR BLESSINGS.

CONTEMPLATE HOW YOU WANT TO BE REMEMBERED.

GRATITUDE IS THE ELIXIR OF LIFE. TELL YOUR FAMILY AND FRIENDS YOU LOVE THEM OFTEN. LIVE YOUR LEGACY, INSTEAD OF JUST BUILDING IT. **ENJOY YOUR MONEY–BUT SPEND WISELY.** PLAN AHEAD. SAVOR YOUR ACCOMPLISHMENTS & CREATE NEW ONES...STRIVE TO BE OPEN-MINDED.

COMMIT TO A LIFETIME OF LEARNING.

GROW A GARDEN, GOLF, HIKE, BIKE, STAY ACTIVE IN WHATEVER YOU CHOOSE. **SMILE,** BE OPTIMISTIC NOT PESSIMISTIC. STAY MENTALLY, EMOTIONALLY, SPIRITUALLY & PHYSICALLY FIT. **THINK** YOUNG TO BE YOUNG. REMEMBER AGE IS ONLY A NUMBER.

STAND STRONG. BE YOUR OWN SOLUTION. DEFINE YOUR FUTURE!

[Source: © Retirement Security Centers, 2013]

Advice from Briggs

After nearly 40 years in the financial planning arena, Briggs offers several pieces of advice to those who are entering into the lifetime income market. He starts by stressing that advisors must become process-driven vs. using a product-centric approach. Whether this entails developing a new method or using an already established system doesn't matter—as long as it is truly objective and easy for clients to follow and engage in.

Another factor that can greatly enhance a new advisor's success is to work in conjunction with a more experienced financial professional. Briggs has adopted this strategy in his own business to better serve his clients and to create a business succession plan.

Knowing that he could not serve so many clients himself, Briggs brought a partner on board about 10 years ago. Jeff Maas, CFP®, ChFC®, CRPC®, is 30 years Briggs' junior. Even without Briggs' lengthy experience in the industry, Jeff has been a great addition—both advisors serve a similar market with a similar mindset. Jeff, a co-founder of the Retirement Security Centers with Briggs, also specializes in meeting the financial planning needs of those who are approaching—or who have already reached—retirement. With Jeff on board, Briggs now knows that his clients and their families are taken care of down the road and that his business will be able to continue serving clients long into the future.

From time to time, Briggs and his team come across clients who "don't so much have a 'running out of money' problem, but rather they have a 'transfer of wealth' problem." A well-developed process will help clients to better understand this and to move forward with recommendations in order to meet their specific financial goals. Clients will be involved in the process and understand their choices and outcomes rather than simply be sold the features and benefits of some product. Product solutions are made to fit the client's situation. When planners stop talking at clients and focus on working with them, a win-win situation is created all around.

For more information on Briggs Matsko, please visit:
www.RetirementSecurityCenters.com.

Briggs Matsko and Jeff Maas are registered representatives of Lincoln Financial Advisors Corp.

Securities and advisory services offered through Lincoln Financial Advisors Corp., a broker/dealer (member SIPC) and registered investment advisor. Insurance offered through Lincoln Marketing and Insurance Agency, LLC and Lincoln Associates Insurance Agency, Inc and other fine companies. Retirement Security Centers is not an affiliate of Lincoln Financial Advisors Corp. CRN 201304-2080074

Key Points

- Make use of an objective, defined process and system.

- Help clients to interactively participate in planning their retirement income strategies.

- Link clients' expenses to specific income-producing sources and assets.

- Combine the use of interactive technology with specific processes to customize a retirement income plan for clients.

- Help clients to ensure that they will never outlive their money.

- Financial planning is not just an event; it is truly an ongoing process.

- Become process-driven versus product-centered.

- Stop talking at clients, and focus more on working with them.

John H. Curry
(Photo courtesy of John H. Curry)

Chapter 2:
The Secure
Retirement
Method

"I help people prepare for a secure retirement,
not a risky retirement."

**John H. Curry, CLU®, ChFC®, AEP®,
MSFS, CLTC**
North Florida Financial Corporation

Years ago, most people looked forward to retirement as a time of rest and relaxation, travel, and doing the things they didn't have time to do while working. Thanks in large part to company pensions, Social Security income, and shorter life expectancies, a majority of retirees did not worry nearly as much about outliving their income.

Fast-forward to today, to a dwindling Social Security fund, uncertain future Medicare benefits, and the complete disappearance of company pension plans. Add in the fact that people are living longer and the result is that the assets and income that retirees do have will be expected to last many more years than in the past. In some cases, individuals will actually spend more years in retirement than they did in the working world.

Some people even believe that the "perfect financial storm" is brewing. As the 78 million Baby Boomers have already started turning 65, what little is currently in the government till won't last much longer. Given the vast amount of expected withdrawals from 401(k)s and other market-related savings vehicles, even the investments that were once thought necessary to beat inflation will likely scare most people away with their heightened volatility.[9]

But John H. Curry, CLU®, ChFC®, AEP®, MSFS, CLTC, of North Florida Financial Corporation understands these worries and helps clients reduce their anxiety about outliving their savings. He puts them in control of their income so they know exactly what is going on with their money. Most people don't plan for retirement properly. In a majority of cases, individuals and couples tend to operate with a relatively high level of financial disorganization. This is because a person's financial picture typically involves a host of insurance policies, legal documents, employee fringe benefits, savings vehicles, debt instruments, and securities products.[10]

People may be required to sift through mountains of information that have been provided by a multitude of institutions and advisors in order to keep their affairs current. Many never accomplish a significant degree of organization and understanding of where they are financially. Those who do will generally only achieve it for an instant and then drift off course again.[11]

John knows all too well the importance of planning for living a long life and covering needs when a life is cut too short—which is one of the key reasons that he initially chose to get into the financial services business.

Born in Texas, John grew up in a small Florida town of only about 300 people. Without much opportunity in his local area, John joined the Air Force, where he quickly learned the importance of planning, using a checklist, and following through. The Air Force is also where he would later craft the idea of the "financial flight simulator" to help clients prepare for their financial futures. As a B-52 Bomber Crew Chief with eight crewmembers' lives in his hands, the concept of responsibility and leadership became crystal clear.

---

9 John H. Curry, Preparing for a Secure Retirement: Expert Insight and Advice on Implementing The Secure Retirement Method (self-published), 2009.
10 John H. Curry, "Secure Retirement Planning," John H. Curry's Secure Retirement Method, 2012, http://johnhcurry.com/.
11 Ibid.

Upon the completion of his Air Force duties, an old high school friend convinced John to join the life insurance business, where he learned and fell in love with the concept of helping people plan for uncertainty.

Little did John know that just a few short years later he would get a firsthand look at just how important life insurance proceeds can be. In 1982, John's brother-in-law committed suicide and, soon afterwards, John's own brother did the same.

It was around that same time that a friend's father began collecting income payments from a retirement annuity — an annuity that John set up. Those checks came in regularly for over 20 years and, upon the man's death, his widow continued to receive income for several years. In total, the couple collected 27 years of payments.

John's key focus, the Secure Retirement Method, engages his clients in clarifying not just their vision but also how they actually feel about retirement. This is an ideal starting point because, while for many, retirement means having the freedom to travel, relax, and have full control over your time, for others it represents being "stuck" with an income that is too small or too uncertain to allow them to do the things that they truly want to do. This can force retirees to continue working in order to make ends meet.[12]

Case Study

John's clients are satisfied because they feel he does the right thing for them.

"I worked with a woman who put eighty percent of her money in a guaranteed interest account and only twenty percent in the market — why? Because she is ultra conservative.

She said to me, 'John, the pain of losing some of my principle is much greater than my desire for gain in the market.'

12 John H. Curry, "The Secure Retirement Method."

> So, as an advisor, what would you do for that woman? You put the money in something safe and secure so that her principal and her interest will not go away. Someone else might say, 'Well, she's only going to get "X" percent interest.' So what? If her fear is losing money then why should she put it at high risk?"[13]

Today, investors are also facing the reality of longer life expectancies. Due to the tremendous advances in medical technology, many people will live to age 100 and beyond. While this is good news for many, it also means that assets and retirement income will be required to last several decades.

Numerous factors need to be considered, including what certain instances could do to your long-term income. Becoming disabled, for instance, can play a number on your finances, especially if you haven't factored in the cost of how this will affect all other areas of your financial life.[14]

Over the years, people methodically do what they think they are "supposed" to do, such as putting funds into their employer's retirement plan or opening an IRA. But this saving is really just the beginning. What really matters is how one will be able to convert those savings over to a sustainable, long-term income in retirement. How this turns out can literally make retirement a time to enjoy or a time to dread. [15]

Example

"I'm going to talk about John and Jane. They are 45 and 42. John is going to retire at 65 and Jane will be 62... John's salary is $40,000, and we assume a three percent pay raise on average. John's average final compensation is projected at $66,000 when he retires, based on an average of his highest five years—not the last five, but the highest five with 33 years of service. John gets the

13 John H. Curry, "Preparing for a Secure Retirement.
14 Ibid.
15 Ibid.

maximum credit for each year, which is 1.68% (33 years x 1.68% = 55.44%)...

What are John's options?

Option 1 would be the maximum for life but upon his death Jane would get nothing. John's benefit is 55% of his average final compensation, $36,685. That's what John would be entitled to. We call that a lifetime pension.

Option 2 is a life income with ten years certain. John retires and gets an income for life. When he dies, what does Jane get? Jane gets ten years and that ten years starts when John retires, not when he dies. The clock starts when you cash the first check... The factor is about 94% of Option 1, $34,000...

Option 3 is joint life with 100% to the survivor. This is 84% of Option 1 for $30,923. People choose this option because they want to take care of their spouse, they want an income for life, and upon their death, they want to make sure their spouse is covered. What happens when they both die? No more money, it dies with them.

Option 4 provides joint life and two thirds to the survivor, that's roughly ninety-four percent, or $34,000. What happens if Jane never worked outside the home and John took Option 4? What would Jane get? Jane gets $22,000. What if Jane dies first? John is reduced down to $22,000. No matter who dies first, the survivor is reduced to two thirds of the original amount.

Which option do you choose? How do you decide?"[16]

It is only when savings, investments, life insurance, and retirement plans are properly coordinated that people will achieve the retirement financial confidence that they hope for. There are also

16 John H. Curry, "Preparing for a Secure Retirement."

several questions that should be answered along the way because every situation is different. For example:

- **"Wealth Building"** – The first step in the overall process is to actually build your wealth. This is because without any assets, there will essentially be nothing to distribute or conserve.

- **"Wealth Distribution"** – There are a number of different moving parts present in this next step, such as determining what happens with your wealth when you pass away. In other words, who is going to get all of the "stuff" you've collected over the years.

- **"Wealth Conservation"** – Rounding out the process is the wealth conservation step. This will involve making sure that all of the assets—as well as all the valuable "stuff"—is protected from certain dangers like taxes, depreciation, and even market losses.[17]

Often, people get nervous when considering these aspects— and they sometimes feel hopeless, in that certain dangers such as market volatility, bad economic times, or even poor financial decisions can erode their lifetime of savings. Yet, the truth is that by creating and implementing a good, solid financial plan, people really do have much more control over their finances.[18]

> When a professor from Florida State University came to John and asked for help in creating a retirement income, John learned everything he possibly could about converting assets into lifetime income.
>
> This experience led John to his primary client focus: retired and retiring members of the Florida Retirement System. Because his father and grandfather worked for the Florida Department of Transportation and John is familiar with Florida's state retirement plans, a large part of John's client base includes individuals and couples who have worked for the Florida school system and state government and are therefore included in the Florida Retirement System. With these clients, John discusses the various options that are available to them.

---

17 John H. Curry, "Preparing for a Secure Retirement."
18 Ibid.

The Secure Retirement Method that John uses focuses on protecting clients' wealth while at the same time providing options to keep retirement income secure in order to preserve and enhance retirees' lifestyles.

Even those who have already done a significant amount of work on their retirement plan can benefit by giving their planning package even more clarity, depth, and creativity. And, those who are starting from scratch will truly appreciate the way that this planning process can help them in accelerating the development of their overall retirement plan.

When implementing John's Secure Retirement Methods, there are four key areas that are covered. These include:

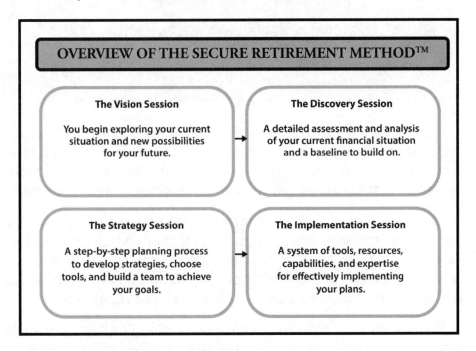

[© 2003–2013 John H. Curry. Overview of the Secure Retirement Method]

When walking clients through the Secure Retirement Method, John uses a "begin with the end in mind" approach to help clients come up with a clear vision of their financial future. He focuses on four primary questions—the first of which gets clients to gain a clear picture of what they want. The following four questions then put into proper perspective the plan that should be created and the actions that must be taken in order to achieve the client's objectives.[19]

The Four Retirement Vision Questions

1. "Think ahead to the day of your retirement. Looking back from that day, what must have happened along the way for you to feel happy about retirement?"

2. "What obstacles and concerns stand in your way to achieving your vision of retirement?"

3. "What are the most important actions that you must take in order to overcome these obstacles and concerns?"

4. "What progress have you already made toward achieving your retirement vision?" [20]

[© 2003–2013 John H. Curry]

Today's lifetime income annuity offers even more options than just simply an income that can't be outlived. Many insurance companies have become more adept at addressing potential client objections and have added optional features to these already great products.

As an example, clients can have their annuity payout increase over time, in essence, keeping up with inflation. Although the client will receive a lower amount of initial income, having an income that rises over time can be very beneficial for those who live a long life or need additional funds for paying healthcare costs later in life.[21]

Some insurance companies are also adding flexibility in lifetime income annuity payment amounts. This can be beneficial for clients who may want more income initially while waiting for Social Security or other retirement income streams to begin, and then wish to lessen the amount that comes in from their annuity when their other income sources start.

---

19 John H. Curry, "Preparing for a Secure Retirement."
20 Ibid.
21 Ibid.

Case Study

John realizes that once someone has enough income to retire, they have the control to pursue hobbies, passions, and all the things that they've dreamed about doing for decades. Without these activities, retirement can be downright depressing.

He notes a series of workshops that he conducted back in 1981 for retirees of General Electric. Many of the attendees needed psychological counseling six months to a year after retirement because they had done nothing throughout their careers except work. They had no outside hobbies or clubs—and absolutely no idea what to do with themselves once their working days were over.

To make matters worse, some of these people were getting divorced from the spouse that they had been with for three or four decades because they had discovered that they really didn't know the person.

These folks literally had to get to know each other again. And it's not just the husband—the wife must adapt, too. The days of the wife staying home and being a "homemaker" are gone. People are different today, which is why it's even more important to have enough in retirement for paychecks and playchecks. Retirement should be thoroughly enjoyed!

John consistently uses the Paychecks and Playchecks strategy, setting up a guaranteed income stream for clients to cover their regular living expenses (or a "paycheck"), along with placing clients' other assets into various investments that can be used for entertainment, vacations, or anything else they choose (a "playcheck").[22]

In his years helping clients plan for a secure retirement, John has noticed several mistakes that people make when planning for that

---

22 John H. Curry, "Preparing for a Secure Retirement."

time in their lives when they won't have employers paying them a steady paycheck. Through workshops and seminars, John teaches his listeners how to plan for and avoid these mistakes.

7 Mistakes Most People Make When Preparing for Their Retirement

1. Underestimating Life Expectancy

2. Paying Too Much in Taxes

3. Not Planning on the Impact of Inflation (The Silent Thief)

4. Relying on Government and Employer Retirement Plans

5. Not Preparing for Healthcare Expenses and Long-Term Care

6. Not Saving Enough on a Personal Basis

7. Focusing on Financial Products Instead of Strategic Planning" [23]

[© 2003–2013 John H. Curry]

John has used the lifetime income annuity strategy for nearly four decades—and has no plans to stop. He has assisted thousands of clients in planning for a secure retirement through his retirement workshops, advisor training sessions, articles, DVDs and CDs, special reports, and personal consultations. Today, John has placed millions in life insurance and annuity premiums, allowing thousands of clients and their loved ones to achieve their financial goals and attain an income stream that they literally cannot outlive.

John's extensive education and experience in financial services has enabled him and his team to provide top-quality service to his clients and associates. He frequently holds informative, educational

23 John H. Curry, "7 Mistakes Most People Make When Planning for Their Retirement," John H. Curry's Secure Retirement Method, 2012, http://johnhcurry.com/mistakes/#.

workshops and seminars on the subject of retirement planning and retirement income distribution.

His professional affiliations include: past-president of the Tallahassee Regional Estate Planning Council, past-president of the Tallahassee Association of Insurance and Financial Advisors, and past-president of the Society of Financial Service Professionals, Tallahassee Chapter. He is active in the Tallahassee Chamber of Commerce, the Sunrise Rotary Club of which he is also past-president, the Marzuq Shrine, and the Boy Scouts of America.

John has also been a member of the Million Dollar Round Table every year since 1980. He credits several mentors for his success, including insurance legends such as Ben Feldman, John Savage, and Tom Wolff. He is also a big fan of the Paychecks and Playchecks method.

I remember one of the first meetings I did for the Guardian Life Insurance Company—John was in attendance. When I finished my talk, he rushed up to talk to me. It was like he found a similar voice in the wilderness. I had just explained the math and science behind what he had been doing for decades! He is one of the early adopters of guaranteed lifetime income—even before he knew all of the "mathematical and scientific" formulas that backed up his recommendations.

I hope you will see a pattern throughout this book: Everyone who studies retirement income eventually gets to the same place. They have to—due to the math and science. However, everyone gets there a different way. And that's what makes it so interesting.

Advice from John

According to John, the truth is that most people already know that they need to save money—and they don't need a financial advisor to tell them that. What they do need is someone who can help them coordinate everything and convert their retirement assets into a lifetime stream of income.

Unfortunately for many investors, following "cookie cutter" advice may only get them average results—or worse. And in some cases, clients just walk away from their money when they leave it with an advisor. It's the advisor's job to make sure that clients pay attention to their statements and stay involved as their financial goals become realities.

He recommends his own successful methods for getting the word out about his strategies—marketing via the Internet. Visitors to his website can sign up to receive more in-depth information on setting up income strategies. They can also receive a free copy of Preparing for a Secure Retirement, which has a focus on the Secure Retirement Method.

His book also helps to position John as an authority in the income planning market, as do his DVD home-study courses. John has created comprehensive courses that focus on retirement income, long-term care, and business succession planning. He offers these courses for sale on his website.

Currently, John has over 3,600 people on his online mailing list. Sending out regular emails helps to keep John's name in front of his clients and prospects. It also provides an avenue to offer updated financial information, as well as to invite clients and prospects to events such as John's golf class and financial reception that he regularly hosts at a local country club.

In addition to working with clients, John also mentors financial service reps who are interested in establishing themselves firmly in the lifetime income annuity market. Once per month, John hosts an agent mastermind group online—learn more at www.AdvisorInnerCircle.com. Agents learn the exact process that makes John's seminars so successful, starting with making a connection with the audience by easing their income-related concerns.

When it comes to leaving a legacy, John says that family comes first. He also believes that telling as many agents about what he does and how he does it can help to exponentially serve the income needs of individuals and couples who fear that their retirement income won't be enough to sustain them throughout the remainder of their lives. Helping people to understand that their financial futures can be in their control—regardless of what the market or the economy is doing—can truly make a world of difference.

For more information about John Curry, please visit www. JohnHCurry.com.

John H. Curry, CLU®, ChFC®, AEP, MSFS®, CLTC – Registered Representative and Financial Advisor of Park Avenue Securities LLC (PAS), 3664 Coolidge Court, Tallahassee, FL 32311. Securities products/services and advisory services are offered through PAS, a Registered Broker-Dealer and Investment Advisor. 1 (850) 562-3000. Financial Representative, The Guardian Life Insurance Company of America (Guardian), New York, NY. PAS is an indirect, wholly owned subsidiary of Guardian. North Florida Financial Corporation is not an affiliate or subsidiary of PAS or Guardian. PAS is a member of FINRA, SIPC.

Key Points

- Begin with the end in mind.

- You can't rely on government sources or company pensions anymore for guaranteed income. Clients must instead create their own secure retirement.

- Many people operate with a relatively high level of financial disorganization.

- You must help clients in clarifying their ideal retirement lifestyle—then you can help them create it.

- Creating retirement income requires an overall holistic and coordinated approach.

- People need someone that can help them coordinate and convert their retirement assets into a lifetime income.

- Use personal experiences—both positive and negative—to shape your future.

- Don't succumb to the many financial myths that surround saving and investing.

- Take advantage of the wide reach of marketing via the internet.

- Position yourself as the expert in the lifetime income annuity area.

Chapter 3: The Ideal Plan Process

John P. Schwan
(Photo courtesy of John P. Schwan)

"No one's ever come to me in the last 30 years and said, 'John, please make sure I'm destitute and broke for my last 15 years' or 'Please make sure that I pay as much income, gift, and estate taxes as humanly possible.' So we focus on creating certainty of income as well as an overall approach that can help in minimizing taxes and enhancing wealth. In many cases, net worth actually has very little to do with the strategy. It's all primarily about creating a steady and guaranteed cash flow."

John P. Schwan
Schwan Financial Group

Most people today are in the mindset that they must continue to save money until "someday" when they retire. They aren't thinking that the real reason they are accumulating all of that savings is to replace their income when the time comes to actually retire. Saving for "someday," though, isn't a defined goal. With guaranteed lifetime income, however, you can put a real date and a real amount of income on that "someday."

John P. Schwan, founder, president, and CEO of Schwan Financial Group, has developed the Ideal Plan Process™, a proven method for defining a client's "someday." Through this process, John is able to custom build a plan that is specifically designed with each individual client's needs in mind. The process also allows all of a client's advisors to work together, essentially creating a much more fluid and coordinated result.

> John, originally from Montana, found an outlet early on for his passion of measurable results through the hard work he put into succeeding in basketball. It even earned him a college basketball scholarship, and the positive results have followed him through his life and career.

> John credits his father, a coach and educator for over 25 years, for his entrance to the financial services business. Both worked as representatives for New York Life until his father's passing at age 54, and both used coaching as a way to increase the effectiveness of their professional life.

In 2002, he was hired as the local high school basketball coach, while already working 15-hour days, 7 days per week as a financial advisor. He found that observation, listening, and specialized attention can make all the difference for the players he coached. That same year, John led New York Life as the number one advisor in the company and his basketball team to a rare state tournament appearance.

According to John, coaching taught him a great deal for his financial services practice: "It's not what you say, but how you say it" that can truly motivate a team—or a client—to the actions necessary in accomplishing their goals. Taking positive and repetitive action can also lead to lifelong good habits.

John's approach to meeting with clients is the same today as it was when he began his financial services career over 30 years ago. He starts by "giving them a good listening to." Taking the time to listen to their wants and concerns solidifies the client-advisor relationship. His methods set him apart from so many other advisors who are more "product" oriented than "process" oriented.

Because most clients do not have a plan for generating the amount of income that they will need in retirement, John asks his clients two simple questions. Together, they move toward a solution by answering the following questions:

- **"Where will your retirement income come from?"**

- **"How long will it last?"**

If they don't have answers, John knows that they need guidance. By implementing a lifetime planning model, he better equips them to answer. With the model, they can plan to have their income needs taken care of for the remainder of their lives, as well as—depending upon how the plan is set up—for the lives of their loved ones.[24]

People would always say that "hindsight is 20/20." For whatever reason, that really bothered John. He kept coming back to it. Finally, he developed a method referred to as the Forward Hindsight process as the foundation of client planning. The "forward" component looks several years into the future and helps clients more clearly envision what their retirement lifestyle would look like. It then walks back to where the client is today and models the potential results of the financial options that are available to the client.[25]

Early on in his career, John learned to ascertain what the most pressing issues on clients' minds were and what kept them up at night. In many cases, the biggest issue was the fear of outliving their retirement income. Knocking on doors, learning what people's key issues were, and asking a lot of questions were daily activities for John.

To further help him and his clients, John dedicated himself to learning everything he possibly could about the financial planning business. In his own words, he "bugged everybody" and asked questions of more experienced advisors.

He also discovered that there is no substitute for activity, as it builds confidence in your own capabilities. So every day he set up a "little blue work card" with all of his prospecting and marketing activities listed. He wouldn't stop for the day until everything was crossed off.

---

24 *LifeStages Lifetime Income Annuity – Now's the Time! Conversations with Tom Hegna and John Schwan*. DVD. 2004.
25 "Your Company," *Schwan Financial Group*, June 2013, http://www.schwanfg.com/company0/.

Today, John still finds the motivation in hard work and determination. While working through the logistics of a client's overall financial plan, John concurrently uses a strategy he has titled "The Clarity Experience." This approach focuses on finding an accurate starting point for the client that uses their current financial situation.

The Clarity Experience helps the client establish the "whys" of their financial planning and goals. Emotional issues are kept in the forefront, so that the technical strategies can mesh with the client's actual reasons for doing what they are doing. By combining the practical with the emotional, he essentially leads them to identify their ultimate goals.

At this stage, a number of issues are brought up and established through his questioning, such as:

- **"Who will be impacted by the client's decisions?"**

- **"When does the client plan for lifestyle and/or business changes?"**

- **"What are the potential consequences to the client's income, taxes, investments, and legacy plans?"** [26]

A written master plan is created. Clients can then better envision and understand how to make decisions that will move them toward their goals and what tools and strategies will get them there.

John's Master Plan Management System clearly demonstrates to the client the importance of acting, executing, implementing, and regularly reviewing the necessary strategies. If a client should ever question why they must continually manage their plan properly, the Master Plan can again be reviewed, reminding the client why their actions are important to their future financial security, their business (if applicable), and their family.[27]

John discovered that by becoming a good listener, clients will essentially tell you exactly what they need. If you can help them solve that need, you can build trust and long-lasting client relationships. He learned these basic tenets by following Wayne Cotton's program for

26 "Introduction Without Interjection," *Schwan Financial Group*, June 2013, www.schwanfg.com/approach1.
27 "Our Approach," *Schwan Financial Group*, June 2013, http://www.schwanfg.com/approach0/.

interviewing potential clients. This program had a huge influence on John as he continued to build his business. It also helped him in creating his own successful systems for fact finding and plan implementation.

By following these same listening steps today, John developed the Ideal Plan Process™—and with great success. His average client case with guaranteed life income needs is in the range of $1 million. Certainly, his focus in this area has paid off. With over 1,400 scheduled events each year, John's business is growing exponentially.

His follow-up statistics are phenomenal, too. At this point, John is only able to schedule one or two retirement income seminars per year because, on average, 95% of the workshop attendees make a follow-up appointment—a good problem to have in any economy!

He is so successful because he covers all of his clients' financial bases with the Ideal Plan Process™. Using a lifetime income annuity in his fixed income strategy has not only helped his clients but has led to success utilizing a wide range of other products and services for his team.

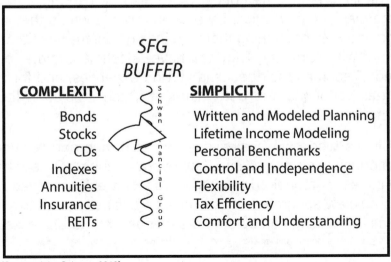

SFG
BUFFER

COMPLEXITY		SIMPLICITY
Bonds		Written and Modeled Planning
Stocks		Lifetime Income Modeling
CDs		Personal Benchmarks
Indexes		Control and Independence
Annuities		Flexibility
Insurance		Tax Efficiency
REITs		Comfort and Understanding

[Source: John Schwan, 2013]

By using a lifetime income annuity, many of his clients will have their fixed income needs covered. Because of this, they are better able to focus on other key areas of planning. Thus, the strategy can help to make all other areas of the financial planning process flow. The reality is that when clients have their basic income needs provided for, all other areas of their life fall into place. When a client has peace of mind in knowing that they will be able to pay regular living expenses—as will their surviving spouse, in cases of married couples—everything else can be more easily coordinated.[28]

In addition, if a client has no need for the income generated, a lifetime income annuity can also be set up to meet other financial goals, such as wealth preservation and stability, family gifting, medical or long-term care costs, and the payment of taxes. Charitable giving goals can also be established and accomplished. These, however, may require consulting with a professional personal tax or legal advisor.[29]

Through the use of an inflation option, you can help to ensure that the guaranteed income from the annuity will regularly increase to give the client future buying power, too. By giving up a little income on the front end, you make up for it over time with increasing income payments.[30]

The lifetime income concept can also be used in a number of estate planning strategies. By showing clients where they currently stand and then combining that with their goals, the clients can move forward with certainty. They will have a lifetime income to pay for "needs," such as their necessary living expenses, and for "wants," such as vacations and entertainment. Such a solution fits ideally into most clients' overall plans.[31]

Clients who own businesses can also incorporate succession and continuity strategies into their overall planning. This is because, oftentimes, personal and family life doesn't exist in a vacuum that is completely separate from the client's business. With this in mind, business planning can be set up either as a stand-alone issue or as

28 *LifeStages Lifetime Income Annuity - Now's the Time! Conversations with Tom Hegna and John Schwan*. DVD. 2004.
29 Ibid.
30 Ibid.
31 "Estate Plan Development and Management," *Schwan Financial Group*, 2012, http://www.schwanfg.com/expertise3/.

a part of the client's Master Plan development.[32]

Whether the client intends to keep their business or sell it, income is typically always their biggest concern. Such unease often affects the business owner, their spouse, and even a long line of dependents. But a lifetime income annuity can be used to successfully address some of their apprehensions.[33]

Along with income-producing strategies, John's team performs an in-depth analysis of clients' situations. Doing so helps clients move closer to their financial goals. In order to achieve optimum tax efficiency, he can also help them recapture overpaid tax dollars and model finances going forward.

Not only can lifetime income annuities add more certainty to one's retirement income, they should automatically satisfy the required minimum distribution (RMD) rules for the annuity—without the need to calculate and withdraw their RMDs. They can be used with both IRA and 401(k) rollovers.

By selecting a 10-year period certain payout option, which is available in many fixed annuties, clients can even have funds guaranteed to pay their beneficiary (or beneficiaries) for up to 10 years, in the case of an early death.[34]

Example

A married couple wants guaranteed income for life. If they purchase a $200,000 joint lifetime income annuity with a cash refund payment option, the husband would receive a check for the remainder of his life, and when he passes away, the wife would get a check in the same amount for the remainder of her life (or vice versa).

But, it doesn't stop there. The couple's family is also protected in the case that both spouses pass away early. For instance, if the husband and the wife both die after receiving only $50,000 in annuity payments, then their

32 "Estate Plan Development and Management," *Schwan Financial Group*, 2012, http://www.schwanfg.com/exper-tise3/.
33 Ibid.
34 *LifeStages Lifetime Income Annuity - Now's the Time! Conversations with Tom Hegna and John Schwan*. DVD. 2004.

> beneficiaries would receive a death benefit in the amount of $150,000.[35]

It's important to let clients know that just because they have an IRA or a 401(k) in their individual name, those funds can be rolled over into a lifetime income annuity for the benefit of both the individual and their spouse—as well as for the benefit of future generations.

Many people have access to employer-sponsored retirement savings programs, such as 401(k)s. A large number of these individuals do a good job of setting aside money for the future on a regular basis. Where the confusion comes in is how to turn those saved dollars into income—income that can allow people to make more choices as to how they spend their retirement.

As most people are aware, at age 70 ½ it is required that they begin taking out a required minimum distribution from their traditional IRA account, 401(k), or any other type of "qualified" money.

But there aren't any taxes due for rolling over funds from an IRA or a 401(k) into an income annuity because technically the annuity will remain inside the IRA account. In addition, there is no 10% withdrawal penalty from the IRS, even if you begin taking your withdrawals prior to age 59 ½. So this strategy can be used for those younger people who want to take an early retirement or an additional guaranteed income stream, as long as you satisfy the substantially equal withdrawal requirement that is governed by Section 72(t) of the Internal Revenue Code.[36]

Section 72(t) of the Internal Revenue Code allows anyone of any age to take substantially equal withdrawals from their qualified money, even if they are below age 59 ½, provided that certain requirements are met.[37]

NOTE: These options need to be discussed with a professional tax or legal advisor to determine if it would make sense for your particular situation.

35 *LifeStages Lifetime Income Annuity - Now's the Time! Conversations with Tom Hegna and John Schwan*. DVD. 2004.
36 Ibid.
37 "Section 72(t)," *Investopedia*, 2013, http://www.investopedia.com/terms/r/rule72t.asp.

For anyone who's age 70 ½ or older, though, an income annuity can essentially allow you to take a larger sum of regular income that doesn't fluctuate in amount—regardless of what the market is doing. And in the current low interest rate environment, this can be significantly more income than a person would receive from a CD.[38]

When designing a long-term financial plan, it isn't simply about planning—but planning well. Likewise, net worth has far less to do with true wealth than cash flow. With this in mind, a lifetime income annuity can easily be implemented to address generational wealth preparedness.

For clients who have achieved wealth—and especially those at a high level—a lifetime income annuity can help to ensure that lifetime income will be received for years down the road. Even grandchildren, great grandchildren, and on down the line can tend to benefit.

If properly structured, these types of annuity products can also help to spread out income for a client's family as well. If the client dies, the children or grandchildren can continue to receive a paycheck, and the income stream would be consistent year after year.

Today, the biggest fear that people have is running out of money. Lifetime income annuities can help solve that problem. John has found various ways to help clients address some of this need for income and certain issues regarding qualified money.

Nationally recognized, John speaks across the country about his processes and philosophy that have helped optimize retirement income planning goals for so many of his clients. At Schwan Financial Group, John and his team are qualified, experienced, and well positioned to help clients plan to realize their goals and objectives by implementing strategies to reach them. They always answer the question, "How can you manage what you cannot measure?" [39]

When I was an annuity wholesaler for New York Life in the late 1990s and early 2000s, John was one of the agents in my territory.

38 *LifeStages Lifetime Income Annuity - Now's the Time! Conversations with Tom Hegna and John Schwan*. DVD. 2004.
39 "Meet The Partners," *Schwan Financial Group*, 2012, http://www.schwanfg.com/team0/.

He was known for writing significant life insurance cases but not many annuities. Aberdeen, South Dakota, is not the easiest place to get to, but I was determined to get in front of him to share some of my ideas.

Time and time again, I tried to set an appointment. Normally, I was just told "no." One time I actually got an appointment, but the week before, I got a call to "reschedule." I was not having any luck. I even spoke at a kickoff meeting for his General Office, but he wasn't able to attend.

In 2002, John attained the council presidency at New York Life. He was the number one agent in the country! Now he had to see me—I was scheduled to speak main platform at all the New York Life council meetings. As the council president, he had to attend all the council meetings and sit through most of the presentations.

Finally, it was my turn on the platform, and I delivered my message on the importance of considering lifetime income as part of clients' overall financial plans. When I looked down to where John had been sitting, his chair was empty! I thought, once again, I'd missed him. Only later was I told that he was in the back of the room for the whole presentation and was very excited about some of the concepts discussed and how these could potentially help his clients. I guess I connected with him.

Within months, John started to use guaranteed lifetime income annuities to help many of his clients obtain a guaranteed fixed stream of income that they could not outlive. With clients that span across numerous states, John often finds himself taking to the air to meet with those who seek his advice on how to best set up a retirement income stream that they won't outlive.

If a client can "see" that their income needs are accounted for— literally for the remainder of their lives—it clears away a great deal of "clutter" and frustration in the client's mind, allowing them to then move toward addressing other goals that are important to them.

The bottom line is that people don't want to be "sold." Rather, they want to make informed decisions. For this reason, John uses modeling in order to clearly show where the client is now and where they will be in the future if they follow the plan.

Going forward, John is focused on his company continuing to age 100 and beyond. He is currently developing a system that will help him accomplish just that! His son has recently joined the business and is learning the many strategies used by his father, including lifetime income strategies and the value that these represent for many clients.

As far as a personal legacy, John wants to be known as an advisor who kept things simple, yet genuinely cared and offered sound advice that helped make a difference in people's lives. When asked what really matters—"I want people to truly feel that we delivered. That's what drives me."

Advice from John

Agents can essentially specialize in just the retirement income market if they choose. Because people's biggest fear is running out of money, financial services professionals who can help clients create a guaranteed fixed income stream that can't be outlived will definitely have a place in the retirement income market.

But before doing so, financial services professionals must learn to be better fact finders. This starts with truly and intently listening. It is here that clients will lay out the road map which can be used to help the clients identify their goals, objectives, and time horizon. From here, a plan can be put into action to help them move toward accomplishing those goals.

John's advice on one of the best ways to initiate client action is to show them where they currently are financially—and then show them what can happen if they do nothing. This alone is a tremendous motivator. After that, compare the results of taking no action with the results they would get by purchasing a lifetime income annuity.

Regardless of anyone's current or future situation, everyone needs cash flow. By being better fact finders, financial professionals will be in a better position to determine what needs to be done to move clients closer to their desired financial goals.

For newer representatives, it is essential to use all the resources that are available. Step back and "know what you don't know." Clients will be much more appreciative of someone who will get back to them later with the correct answer than someone who plows forward, possibly in the wrong direction.

Most financial product providers have consultants who can assist the financial professionals with their understanding of how certain financial and insurance products work, what features they offer, and the potential benefits of owning the product for clients with a particular profile, as well as the necessary paperwork to get the product implemented.

John rarely gets objections from the individuals and couples who he shares his proposed guaranteed lifetime income strategy with.

But when he does, it is typically because the client may want more "cushion" in the form of liquidity.

These concerns can be addressed by ensuring that no single option is used to address clients' needs using 100% of a client's available funds. Once clients are well positioned to have enough income to cover their living expenses—along with some additional disposable funds that can be used for other goals—they typically move forward with the recommended strategy.

It all comes down to fact finding and discovering the possible alternatives available to fund their needs. People are attracted to certainty—today more than ever. Creating a fixed income stream through a lifetime income annuity can provide a certain degree of comfort for many clients.

How much less risk would people take if they knew with certainty that they didn't need to be completely invested in the market in order to be financially secure? Using a lifetime income annuity allows clients to invest a portion of their funds much more conservatively and safely.

For additional information about John Schwan, please visit: www.schwanfg.com.

This section represents a general overview of how John Schwan started his career in financial services and how certain principals, training, and experience have helped him to be effective in the area of retirement income planning. Neither John Schwan nor Schwan Financial Group is affiliated with the author, Tom Hegna. Nothing in this Chapter is to be considered an offer of any specific product or service, nor is it intended to provide any specific tax advice. Readers are advised to consult a professional focused in the areas discussed to help them address their specific situation.

Key Points

• Talk to your clients and truly listen to their concerns and what they are trying to accomplish. Building client trust is more important than anything else.

• Create your habits and your habits will create you. Most people are attracted to certainty. Creating cash flow through a lifetime income annuity can help provide some of that certainty that many clients are seeking.

• Help clients see and evaluate where they currently are financially—and then show them what can happen if they do nothing.

• Lifetime income annuities can offer many attractive features and benefits depending on the client's specific needs and situation.

• Use your resources to obtain additional information on the various alternatives available to discover the answers that you may not yet have.

PART TWO

STRATEGIES

John Olsen
(Photo courtesy of John Olsen)

Chapter 4:
An Annuity is Not an Investment, It's an Income Stream

"Clients are worried that their account balance will fall to zero before their blood pressure does."

John Olsen, CLU®, ChFC®, AEP®
Olsen Financial Group

Although risk is a simple, four-letter word, it really is not very well understood. Usually holding a negative connotation, risk does not always have to be unpleasant. We face risk every day; financial risk is just a part of life—but we don't have to agonize over it. With an increased life expectancy combined with a volatile market, the biggest risk that retirees face today is running out of money.[40]

John L. Olsen, CLU®, ChFC®, AEP®, an insurance agent and estate planner practicing in St. Louis County, Missouri, strives to reduce his clients' anxiety. Understanding risk, he uses various techniques and methods for designing income projections and strategies to help reduce or eliminate this risk.

John began to understand the concept of risk through the study of history, graduating from the University of Missouri at Columbia in 1968 with a Bachelor of Arts. Following graduation, he did graduate work in

40 John L. Olsen, "Longevity Annuities Could Redefine the Retirement Income Landscape," *LifeHealthPro*, January 1, 2009, http://www.lifehealthpro.com/2009/01/09/longevity-annuities-could-redefine-the-retirement.

history and education, where he learned the power of preparation and thorough research. Since 1973, John has been involved in the financial services industry, starting as a life insurance agent with MetLife. He faced risk every day as he made cold calls to newly married couples for the purpose of offering them whole life insurance.

John readily admits that cold calling was a formidable process, remembering one particular week where he had 14 appointments set—half of them stood him up, the other half said no. It was then that John came to the conclusion that new life insurance agents must "solicit rejection on a daily basis."

One vehicle that will allow clients to receive an income that they can't outlive is the annuity. These financial instruments can provide clients peace of mind; they know that their income will continue indefinitely. They eliminate the worrisome risk that they will live longer than their portfolio.

But there is one catch—when clients opt for the life only payout option, there is the potential that some or all of the funds they deposit will not be returned, should they die early on.

John initially started to focus on the retirement income market for two primary reasons. One, the retirement income problem is both complex and interesting, so it intrigued John as an academic. The second reason was that to John, focusing on a problem that's going to face us all at some point simply made good business sense.

In 1978, John transferred from a sales manager position with Metropolitan Life to director of training for the St. Louis agency of Lincoln National Life. He then moved on to General American Life in 1985 as the regional marketing and sales consultant for the St. Louis (MO) region. Filled with valuable experiences and new ideas, John left General American in 1987 to start his own financial consulting practice, Olsen Financial Group, where he focuses on estate planning for clients as well as writing, teaching, and consulting. In 2010, John joined Jack Marrion, a nationally known expert on index annuities, to form Olsen & Marrion, LLC, which in that year published their book, *Index Annuities: A Suitable Approach*.

Fascinated with annuities as an income-producing instrument, John came to the conclusion that once a client's "must-have" income needs are taken care of, they can make other discretionary income choices more easily. In his educational presentations, John makes the point that, as agents do lifetime income planning with clients, they are faced with two "unknowables." First, what future investment returns will be and in what order they will occur. Second, how long the income produced by the client's portfolio must last (because nobody knows how long they will live).

The longevity annuity (also known as the "deferred income annuity") is a type of income annuity, as discussed in depth in the chapter on Curtis Cloke. By putting all the mortality credits at the end of life, this tool takes longevity risk—John's second "unknowable"—off the table. This allows advisors to manage the client's remaining money differently, while also allowing clients to spend more on lifestyle expenses, such as vacations, that they might have foregone without the assurance of late-life income from the longevity annuity.

Traditional advisors who use mutual funds and managed money can find a longevity annuity attractive, since less money is needed; therefore, more of the portfolio remains as assets under management (AUM). Believe it or not, there are still advisors who are concerned about "committing annuicide" to their AUM by using annuities, even though study after study has documented that those advisors using lifetime income annuities actually gain assets. By doing the right thing for clients, advisors gain the clients' trust, making the clients invest more money with them and refer many more friends and relatives. Plus, the pressure on the rest of the portfolio is reduced.

Example

Tom, age 60, places a small portion of his retirement savings into an annuity. Once he reaches a specified age — in this case, 85 — the annuity will provide a guaranteed income for the rest of Tom's life.

The income that Tom receives will likely be far more than can be assured by any other investment alternative. A single deposit of $50,000 at age 60 will produce a guaranteed income of just over $3,200 per month when Tom reaches age 85, regardless of what interest rates do or what happens in the market.

But if Tom dies before he reaches age 85, the annuity would expire without value. Based on this fact, there are many clients and advisors who balk at the thought of taking on this "investment" risk — buying a policy that won't pay the client a penny for 25 years and, if he doesn't live that long, losing his entire investment.[41]

This "investment objection" would be accurate if the longevity annuity were an investment. But it isn't. It is a pure risk transfer instrument. The risk that the client is transferring to the insurance company is the possibility that he will live past age 85, outliving his income. If he does, the annuity will pay him the stated amount of income — regardless of what happens to interest rates — for as long as he lives.[42]

It should be noted that in some versions of the longevity annuity, the annuitization age may be chosen in advance and a death benefit (payable if the purchaser dies before the annuitization age) is available. Obviously, the annuity benefit is greater for the "no death benefit" version.

Remember also that you can purchase lifetime income annuities that continue to pay a spouse or child an income for as long as they live as well. Plus, there are other guarantees like cash refund, period certain, installment refund, and even a percentage of premium death

41 Olsen, "Longevity Annuities Could Redefine."
42 Ibid.

benefit. Just realize that the more money you want guaranteed, the lower the paycheck will be.

One of the biggest objections to a longevity annuity is the perception that the buyer will die shortly after purchasing one. In this case, says the objection, the insurance company "keeps" the client's money.

There are two counters to that objection. First, as John says, "Dead people don't need income!" The risk of running out of money in extreme old age never materializes if you don't live that long. The second counter is to correct the misconception that the insurance company "keeps the money." It doesn't; it pays that money to those annuity holders who live longer than expected.

This concept is what is referred to as mortality credits—and it's what gives annuities the ability to pay out income for a longer period of time to those who live long lives. Technically, with a participating annuity, the premiums that are paid by those who die earlier than expected will actually contribute to gains of the overall risk pool. Thus, they provide a higher yield, or credit, to survivors than could be achieved through individual investments that lie outside of the annuity risk pool.

In addition, mortality credits increase with a client's age—and they can actually be used to hedge the risk of longevity. This fact is what allows annuities to provide a return that would literally be impossible to match in the broader financial markets.

When explaining this concept to clients, however, there is a much better way to keep it simple: help them understand that they are simply transferring the risk that they will live a long life to the insurance company. Either way—if they die young or live to be 100, their income needs will be taken care of for the rest of their life.

Offering and purchasing longevity annuities, then, is an issue of perception. For advisors who are stuck on the issue of a client "losing their money" if they die too soon, the perception must be redirected to a "transfer of risk" viewpoint, which recognizes that longevity annuity purchasers don't actually "give up" their funds; they simply swap these dollars for a future stream of income.

Both agents and clients must stop applying investment mentality to a risk transfer instrument. The misconceptions about longevity and immediate annuities must be corrected. Once that happens, the true costs and benefits will be much clearer.

> John is a sought-after speaker for his understanding of risk and annuities, giving presentations throughout the country to recognized industry associations and professionals. He has appeared as a panelist in two of the Society of Financial Service Professionals' nationally distributed video teleconferences.

> John is a past-president of the St. Louis chapter of the National Association of Insurance and Financial Advisors (NAIFA) and currently serves on the Boards of Directors of the St. Louis Estate Planning Council and the St. Louis Chapter of the Society of Financial Service Professionals (SFSP). He is also a member of the editorial advisory board of Tax Facts.

I met John over 10 years ago when I spoke at a meeting in St. Louis. He was an enthusiastic listener, to say the least. He asked questions throughout the meeting and added input whenever something was missing. I knew right away that this guy really knew his stuff. His books, *Index Annuities: A Suitable Approach* and *Taxation and Suitability of Annuities for the Professional Advisor*, should be on the shelves of every serious annuity producer; I often use them myself as references.

> John has written and taught courses in insurance, financial, and estate planning and conducted seminars for agents, planners, and lay audiences. In addition to serving his own clients, John provides consulting services to attorneys, accountants, insurance agents, and financial advisors. He is frequently called upon to be an expert witness in various court cases involving finance and insurance situations.

> In 2010, John published *Index Annuities: A Suitable Approach* (www.indexannuitybook.com) with co-author Jack Marrion. In 2012, Olsen & Marrion published John's

newest book, *Taxation and Suitability of Annuities for the Professional Advisor*. Also in 2012, John completed with co-author Michael E. Kitces the third revised edition of *The Advisor's Guide to Annuities*, a book for professional advisors published by the National Underwriter Company.

He has also written articles on life insurance, annuities, planning software, and financial and estate planning topics for many prominent industry publications and has been quoted in such publications as the Wall Street Journal, Forbes, and Barron's. His article "Annuities and Suitability: Reflections on the State of the Debate," published in the November 2006 issue of the Journal of Financial Service Professionals, won the first place prize in the 2006 Kenneth Black, Jr. Journal Author Award Program.

John's message is that, in reality, "the nature of annuities is simple".[44] They are primarily risk transfer devices, not investments, although some types of annuities certainly have investment characteristics. Investment logic, all by itself, will not discover their value. Indeed, some annuities—longevity annuities in particular—can be best understood as property or liability insurance. If the "insured peril" occurs (the buyer reaches age 85), the insurance pays off; if not, there's no payoff.

We insure our homes and automobiles because their loss would cause us hardship, but we don't expect a return on investment for those premium dollars. If our car or home isn't destroyed while we have them insured, we've lost nothing, for we had the assurance that they would be restored with the insurance proceeds.[43]

In a similar fashion, if clients were to "insure" their longevity and their need for income using just a small portion of their total wealth, that insurance would not have been in vain. They would receive the confidence to spend the remainder of their money on other things in life. Thus, the real value of annuities is not just in the income that they provide, but in the life choices that they can make possible.[44]

43 Olsen, "Longevity Annuities Could Redefine."
44 Ibid.

Advice from John

For those who wish to use immediate annuities with clients, John has several tips that can help agents get up to speed successfully. First, fully understand exactly what it is that you are offering, especially as it relates to a comprehensive planning approach.

As a big fan of education, John stresses that agents should read everything they can possibly get their hands on about annuities— including taking Continuing Education courses. This also includes reading the entire annuity contract prior to offering it to a client. John stresses that if you haven't read the contract, you have no business selling it. You can never learn too much! In addition, having a mentor and doing joint work together can also be extremely beneficial.

It goes without saying that agents must do what is in the client's best interest—no exceptions. A big part of that is being aware of all the client's other financial holdings. Be aware of licensure issues, too. In some states, if a client will be selling securities in order to fund the annuity, the agent must have a securities license.

When showing illustrations to clients, John suggests showing them both with and without the cost of living adjustment. This dual perspective will give the clients the option to choose which one they feel the most comfortable with.

In addition, if using a deferred annuity, always tell the client about the annuity's surrender charge. This is key, as there will be times when clients may panic at the thought of locking up their funds—even in return for the promised stream of income. In any case, have the client document the life only payout option if they choose to go this route. Properly understood, surrender charges are owner benefits, not drawbacks. They permit the insurer to credit more interest (from investments in longer-term bonds) than it could have, absent those charges.

It is essential to always ensure that the client fully understands the payout and the concept that they have not given up a large chunk of money, but have merely exchanged it for a regular and ongoing stream of income.

The fact that clients' income needs can be taken care of for the rest of their lives is truly an emotional issue. For this reason, John asks his clients to close their eyes and visualize a check arriving regularly, month after month, year after year, for the rest of their lives.

For more information about John Olsen and his Index Annuities, please visit:

www.indexannuitybook.com

Key Points

- Risk is not very well understood.

- The biggest risk that retirees face today is running out of money before they run out of time.

- The need for future income is challenging, as nobody knows exactly how long they are going to live.

- An annuity is not an investment—it is a risk transfer vehicle.

- Mortality credits allow those who live longer to receive income via the assets of those who die early.

- Because of mortality credits, annuities can provide a return that would be impossible to match with other types of financial tools.

- Both agents and clients must stop applying investment mentality to risk transfer instruments.

- Always ensure that annuity clients fully understand the payout and the surrender charges.

- The real value of annuities is in the choices that they can make possible.

Chapter 5: Income Annuities in the Context of Holistic Retirement Management

Michael Gordon
(Photo courtesy of Michael Gordon)

"In retirement, clients need to maintain a steady income stream beyond their Human Capital. Basic expenses, discretionary expenses, legacy objectives, and additional goals can all be met with [guaranteed lifetime income]." [45]

Michael Gordon
Longbridge Investments LLC

Everyone has different financial needs—from savings to investments to protection of assets—and these needs tend to change as people pass through different stages of their lives. Young couples and parents, for example, worry that their loved ones may not be able to survive, or at least not survive very well, if a breadwinner's income is suddenly lost. It is for this reason that many people purchase life insurance.

Likewise, as people approach retirement, their focus begins to shift somewhat to a need to survive, as they are no longer receiving income from their employer. Given today's increase in life expectancy, these individuals have very valid concerns regarding outliving their assets. The good news is that these consumers can benefit by converting at least some of their savings into lifetime income through immediate annuities.

Michael Gordon, co-founder and managing partner of Longbridge Financial, has a special affinity for products that help retirees manage

45 Michael Gordon, "Reaching the Affluent Market through Lifetime Wealth Strategies" (presentation).

longevity risk. Michael in particular likes products such as lifetime income annuities that offer economically superior results while at the same time offer peace of mind to consumers.

His affinity for insurance began at birth: The insurance industry runs in Michael's blood. His father, George Gordon, was one of the top managers in New York Life history. Tragically, Michael's father passed away at a young age in 2009 from ALS, the devastating disease more commonly known as Lou Gehrig's disease. Michael described the debilitating disease like "being buried alive," as your mind remains unaffected but your body wastes away as your muscles atrophy.

Because George was such an industry legend, and because he helped so many people throughout his career, his death was felt by many.

Although they could not be prepared for the emotional toll that the disease would take, Michael's family was lucky enough to have done the proper planning. They could afford to care for George at home, and Michael's mother would never have to worry about money.

This experience reinforced for Michael his already strong belief in risk pooling products. Not only does he acknowledge their academic soundness and the macroeconomic benefit, he profoundly appreciates the impact that these products have on individual families, the quality of their lives, and the comfort of their final days.

To Michael, the biggest lesson he took from this experience was that he saw his father work his entire life for the security of his family. Having guaranteed income in place for his wife following his passing allowed Michael's father to die with some peace in his heart that his life's work would mean something. That it would provide security to those he loved; that, even though he would not be there anymore, he could continue to provide financial security for the love of his life.

From his early experience, Michael discovered many advantages of the lifetime income annuity. In addition to offering a guaranteed income for life, such annuities have another key advantage: they can generate a higher level of sustainable income than other types of investments in similarly risky assets can.

What generates this superior income? Some annuity purchasers will die prior to life expectancy and others will live much longer than expected. Insurance companies can use the risk pool generated by this dynamic to enhance payout rates to all their customers. These excess payments are referred to as mortality credits—and all lifetime income annuities have them.

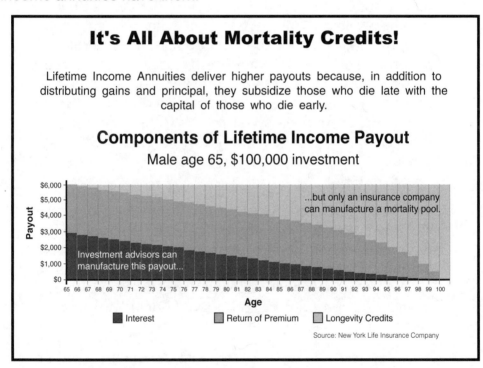

In the most basic sense, mortality credits are what allow income annuities to provide income for their holders for the remainder of their lives, regardless of how long that may be. The life insurance company takes the premiums that are paid by those who die earlier than expected and contributes them to the income of those clients in the "pool" who live longer than expected. It is this method that allows for the additional income above what traditional investments can safely generate in the course of a lifetime of uncertain duration.

With this framework in mind, then, the longer annuity holders live, the more mortality credits they will get.

Michael discovered over the years that lifetime income annuities provide both psychological and economic benefits that traditional investments can't provide.

> Until early 2012, when he founded Longbridge Financial, Michael spent most of his career at New York Life Insurance Company. Over the years, he gained increasing responsibility for driving corporate strategy, new product innovation, and a variety of capacities that would help agents develop effective solutions for their clients. Michael officially served as senior vice president and head of Agency-Life Operations, an organization that comprised a significant portion of New York Life's career agency-distribution system and pricing and product manufacturing for the US Life Insurance Business, as well as the Retirement Market, the Registered Investment Advisor, and the Broker Dealer.

> He was one of the inventors for the development of "methods and systems for providing longevity insurance with or without an asset-based premium [to] determine an appropriate premium and income payment amounts when issuing income-generating products to clients." Michael's work at New York Life also included developing proprietary programs, including lifetime income annuities.

> In his last role at New York Life, Michael served as senior vice president and head of new business ventures for New York Life Enterprises. His responsibilities included developing business plans and leading new businesses for the company.

Having developed his lifelong passion for insurance into a portfolio of potential product and distribution solutions for the US retirement crisis, Michael left New York Life in 2012 to form Longbridge Financial.

His is a finance company and fund with a focus on using housing wealth to generate lifetime income. Longbridge also has a focus on taking a more holistic view of different markets and asset classes in order to hedge clients' risk. Michael is particularly interested in helping people transform their housing wealth into lifetime income through reverse mortgage products. He strives to build on his work of incorporating illiquid, non-traditional assets into portfolios to help investors achieve superior risk-adjusted returns.

Michael and his company work on the premise that longer-term, consumer-oriented financing solutions will continue to increase in relevance over time.

> Over the years, Michael has been involved in a number of different areas of the insurance arena—including product management, actuarial, and operations. In doing so, he has managed more than 500 employees. Michael has been able to provide advisors with a wide vareity of different technological tools and techniques that can help advisors move their clients toward their retirement income goals.[46]

> Prior to serving as head of the company's life business, Michael served in various capacities at New York Life, including the Corporate Internet Department, the Business Resilience Department, the Individual Annuity Department, and the Career Agency Distribution Department.

Although Michael does not work directly with clients, in many ways he can actually be considered the "advisor's advisor." Behind every great advisor is someone who gives them the tools to be great. Michael has been that guy for many advisors; he really helped me drive lifetime income annuity sales when we were both at New York Life.

I always said that Michael was the "PhD" and I was the kindergarten teacher. Michael would come up with all of the serious and complicated reasons to prove that these products were superior.

---

46 "About Us." Longbridge Financial, 2013, https://longbridge-financial.com/about-us/leadership.

Although there is a great deal of math and science behind the inner workings of annuities, I stressed that when explaining them to clients, the key is to keep things simple.

I have been in the insurance industry for 25 years and I have met tens of thousands of people. I can say that Michael Gordon may very well be the most brilliant company officer that I have ever had the pleasure of working with. He worked behind the scenes for years as an assistant vice president and corporate vice president at New York Life. Once his outstanding performance was recognized by senior management, he was quickly promoted to senior vice president.

Let me put it this way: I was senior to Michael for a number of years, and, not very long after, he was senior to me. What makes Michael so special is not just that he knows a lot—and he does. It is that he does so much with that knowledge. When Michael does something, he really does his homework! He developed key relationships with the brightest research people in the industry—people from Morningstar and Ibbotson. He even called and spoke directly to the "Father of Lifetime Income," Dr. Menahem Yaari in Israel! When we worked together on the Lifetime Income Annuity Initiative, I would tell Michael the kind of materials we needed—illustrations, marketing material, etc.—and within days, I would have a product in my hand! It was truly amazing.

Advice from Michael

While it's important that annuity purchasers understand exactly where their money is going, the real purpose of the lifetime income issue is the fact that having a continuous cash flow allows people to pay their living expenses. They can then make clearer choices about other aspects of their life that they may not otherwise have been able to accomplish.

In fact, when compared with using only traditional assets, there are quite a few differences—especially when it comes to accumulation and decumulation and the primary risks that are addressed.

Simplicity also works when closing the sale. For example, rather than providing clients with one cut-and-dried, yes-or-no solution, it is oftentimes easier for clients to choose between two alternatives—in other words, give them an "A or B" choice rather than a "yes or no."

Certainly, even for those clients who love the concept of the lifetime income annuity, it is important that clients not put all of their money into one single product. It makes much more sense to leave at least some assets in vehicles with higher growth potential in order to help maintain purchasing power in the face of potential future inflation.

**For additional information regarding Michael Gordon and
Longbridge Financial,
visit: www.longbridge-financial.com**

Key Points

• In addition to offering a guaranteed income for life, annuities can generate a higher level of sustainable income than many other types of investments—even ones that are in higher yielding underlying investments.

• By using mortality credits, insurance companies essentially pass along money that would have gone to annuity holders who pass away early to those who are still living.

• Advisors who use solutions that integrate traditional and non-traditional assets can create customized solutions that will provide better outcomes for their clients.

• Even if a lifetime income annuity is beneficial to a client, you should not put "all of their eggs in one basket."

• Although there is a great deal of math and science behind the inner workings of annuities, when explaining them to clients, the key is to keep things simple.

Chapter 6: Cinderella Slipper Strategies

John W. Homer
(Photo courtesy of John Homer)

"These are the only strategies about which I know where people purchase large amounts of life insurance and have better cash flow after the purchase than before. They don't fit all feet, but where they fit, they turn a Cinderella situation into a princess situation with a very happy ending."

John W. Homer, CLU®
Oxford Financial Group

Annuities can be thought of as being the "opposite" of life insurance. With life insurance, people typically pay premiums on a regular basis to cover a lump sum benefit that will go to their beneficiaries should they "die too soon." On the other hand, with annuities, people generally deposit funds into an account that will later pay them income on a regular basis, which essentially protects them from "living too long" and outliving their assets.

John W. Homer, CLU®, president and chairman of Oxford Financial Group and a Chartered Financial Consultant with over 30 years of experience, explains that there is really only one similarity between life insurance and a guaranteed income annuity: the contracts end when the person dies. Since he uses a combination of life insurance and annuities, John usually uses life only or joint life only. For his strategies, the life insurance would kick in at death.

John has had phenomenal success using the combination of income annuities and life insurance strategies with his clients. But it wasn't always easy. After graduating from college with a business degree, John joined the Air Force—during the Vietnam era.

Upon leaving the military, John decided to enter the financial services market, getting his start at Beneficial Life. Admittedly not a fast starter in the insurance and financial services business, John says that he often had bigger balances on his credit cards than on his W-2.

Finally, after about eight years, something clicked when John got into the 401(k) market. By targeting municipalities that were opting out of Social Security, John designed a Social Security replacement package that earned him numerous referrals. Finally, he began to enjoy the fruits of his labor, specifically in the estate planning and business market.

By the 1990s John had worked with many business owners and turned his focus to helping them with their business and estate planning. In the estate planning area, John has developed several unique strategies that are not part of most traditional estate plans.

John has noticed that some of his most successful clients are more concerned about what inherited wealth may do "to" their children rather than what it may do "for" them. These people have seen what other families have experienced when children inherit wealth they did not earn and were unprepared to receive.

In traditional estate planning, the process usually focuses on reducing or eliminating estate and inheritance taxes. While John still helps his clients avoid unnecessary taxes, he and his team provide their clients with a strategy known as the Legacy Planning Process. Through this unique, five step procedure, they assist clients by focusing on the following areas of discovery:

1) **"Seeing Their 'Current Future'"** – A client's "current future" goes far beyond just what one's estate will look like in terms of net worth and taxation. John and his team take a good hard look at the client's estate distribution and the effect such a distribution will have on the client's loved ones. They also explore the possibilities

of specific causes and charitable organizations that the client cares about.

The key issue is determining how today's state of affairs will actually translate into tomorrow's reality. To do so, John asks his clients to fill out his Legacy Questionnaire. By doing so, clients must quantify their feelings about wealth, define what it means to them, and make clear what they want the fruits of their labor to accomplish in the future. The questionnaire also helps them face non-financial issues, both current and future.

2) **"Limiting Taxes"** – In this phase, John and his team show clients how they can limit their estate and capital gains taxes and how, in some cases, they can reduce their current income tax liability. Here, too, they involve the client in the overall process through the use of a short questionnaire.

3) **"Preserving Control and Lifestyle"** – John and his team don't want their clients to view estate planning as a negative process of giving everything away. Instead, they strive to ease that fear and transform it into control—to see estate planning as a means of preserving the lifestyle that their clients are accustomed to.

4) **"Crafting an Appropriate Inheritance"** – In crafting an appropriate inheritance, John helps clients balance the delicate proportion of giving enough to fund ample opportunities for heirs without accidentally passing on such a large inheritance that it ends up allowing them to choose an unproductive life.

5) **"Extending Their Reach"** – John also works with clients to preserve that which the client values the most, thereby constructing a way for the client to be remembered.[47]

The successful completion of these five phases creates a very different result than the "current future" his clients discover in the first phase of the Legacy Planning process. In order to ensure completion of the planning process, John has learned that a team approach is absolutely necessary. He accomplishes this by working with his clients' other professional advisors.

47 "The Oxford Five Phase Planning Process," Oxford Financial Group, Inc., June 2013, http://www.oxfordfinancialgroup.com/oxfordfinancialgroup.aspx?MyMenu=home&MyPage=freeform.asp&SessionID-116000416.

Two of the many tools that John uses are his Legacy Questionnaire and a series of strategies that he refers to as Cinderella Slipper Strategies.

The Legacy Questionnaire consists of a several dozen questions designed to provoke thought about the client's future. Because most traditional estate planning revolves around discussions of taxes and net worth, John wants his clients to think in terms of their True Wealth. True Wealth is the combination of Core Assets, Character Assets, Contribution Assets, and Capital Assets. John's process assists families in discovering, enhancing, and optimizing all the assets that comprise their True Wealth.

How people leave their wealth often says more about who they are, or were, than how they used their wealth during their lifetime. Some of the questions in his Legacy Questionnaire include:

• "If you were examining your family 20 years after your passing, what must have happened in order for you to be happy with your planning? What if the examination takes place 100 years after your passing?"

• "How do you keep your net worth from poisoning your True Wealth?"

• "What is the purpose of your wealth?"

• "How do you provide tools instead of toys?"

• "How can you empower children to reach their dreams?" [48]

As part of his planning, John helps his clients increase their spendable cash flow. Several of the strategies that John and his team use have regularly produced guaranteed incoming cash flows of between 4% and 7% in an otherwise 3% to 5% interest rate environment.

Clients hoping to increase their cash flow may, or may not, be estate planning clients. With interest rates being so low, most people are interested in discovering ways in which they can receive a decent guaranteed cash flow from their liquid assets.

48 "Searching Questions," Oxford Financial Group, Inc., June 2013, http://www.oxfordfinancialgroup.com/oxfordfinancialgroup.aspx?MyMenu=home&MyPage=freeform10.asp&SessionID=205544422.

John values what he preaches, and incorporates his professional life into his personal. He is past-president of the Salt Lake City Estate Planning Council and has served as chairman of the Primary Children's Medical Center Planned Giving committee. He has also served as president of the Utah Chapter of the Society of Financial Service Professionals and is a past-president of the Utah State Association of Insurance and Financial Advisors.

I was fortunate to meet John a few years ago when I spoke at the Grant Taggart Symposium in the Salt Lake City/Provo (UT) area. A founder of the symposium, John ensures that it is a top-shelf meeting every year, typically bringing in MDRT-level speakers to share the latest in cutting-edge sales ideas for advisors.

I then got a chance to see John at the 2012 MDRT annual meeting in Anaheim, where he gave an incredible speech, titled "The Cinderella Slipper Strategies." After explaining many of his strategies, he described the ideal client and compared his strategies to Cinderella's glass slipper: "They don't fit all feet, but where they fit, they turn a Cinderella situation into a prince or princess with a very happy ending."

The ideal client that fits these methods—or "feet"—is generally between age 70 and age 90 and has available liquid assets that can be put toward the income generation plan. In addition, these clients will typically also want to accomplish at least one of the following goals:

- "Increase cash flow from their liquid assets"

- "Remove assets from their taxable estate"

- "Create an economic engine for charitable trusts which guarantees 100% asset replacement, instead of the declining balance that is typical in such instruments"

- "Eliminate estate and IRD taxes on qualified monies"

- "Produce more cash flow after they purchase large amounts of life insurance than they had before they made the purchase"

• "Ease—and eventually erase—the income tax liability that is found in older types of deferred annuity contracts"[49]

Such strategies use a guaranteed income annuity tool—sometimes referred to as a single premium immediate annuity (SPIA). Specifically, they use this product with a life only payout option in order to maximize the amount of income that is received.

> In the mid-1990s, John attended a conference where he learned some incredible strategies on how to use SPIAs in conjunction with life insurance coverage.

> Wondering why the speaker—a top producer at the time—would spill all of his planning strategies, John later found out that the presenter had terminal cancer and wanted to help as many other advisors as possible.

> Thankful for the wisdom, John used these same techniques to catapult himself to even more success in the industry. Due to such success, John was able to create his own company, one that specializes in assisting families with specific areas of both financial and estate planning.

When working with guaranteed income annuities, John does not refer to the payout from the annuity as income, but as cash flow. This is because the word income oftentimes implies taxable cash flow.

Unlike income, the cash flow that comes from these types of annuities is not always fully taxable. In fact, in the early years of the payout phase, the majority of the cash flow is generally tax free because it is the return of the client's principal.

Opposed to other traditional investments, the cash flow that is achieved is not determined by interest rates but rather by the age and estimated life expectancy of the client. Again, we can see mortality credits at work, providing additional funds—and return—for those who live longer.

49 John W. Homer, *Cinderella Slipper Strategies: Utilizing the Forgotten Tool* (2012).

The payout of the annuity is meant to return the total amount that was paid to purchase it plus some interest and mortality credits. Such a payout is calculated to be spread out over the annuitant's life expectancy. Therefore, depending on how long the person lives, the annuitant might actually receive more or less than what they paid for the original premium. And, the older the annuitant is, the shorter the life expectancy is.

With this in mind, older annuitants will receive a greater amount of payout, or cash flow, from the annuity than younger annuitants. In addition, the cash flow for males will be higher than for females because males' life expectancy is typically shorter.

To reiterate, each payment that comes from an annuity will be divided into three distinct parts. These are:

- "return of initial premium (tax free)"
- "interest earnings (subject to income tax)"
- "mortality credits (subject to income tax)" [50]

Clients can also get some tax advantages when receiving annuity income, because at least a portion of each payment is actually a return of the client's original deposit. The percentage of the income payment that is considered a return of principal is referred to as the annuity's exclusion ratio.

Over time—and especially for those who live longer—all of the original premium will be paid out to the annuitant. At this point, any additional income that is received will be considered gain and will therefore be taxable as income to the recipient. This also includes the income that is received from mortality credits. [51]

John notes that as clients and advisors look at the payout rates, it is important to view the annual cash flow coming from the annuity as a percentage of the amount that was used to purchase that cash flow.

"This cash flow is NOT the interest rate earned or credited to

50 Homer, Cinderella Slipper Strategies.
51 "8% Cash Flow in a 3% Market," Oxford Financial Group, Inc., June 2013, http://oxfordfinancialgroup.com/oxfordfinancialgroup.aspx?MyMenu=home&MyPage=freeform8.asp&SessionID=110886346.

the account. It is NOT taxable income. It is NOT yield. It is strictly the rate that cash is flowing from the contract based on the initial premium and the cash being paid out." [52]

Once prospective clients understand the concept of guaranteed cash flow, John receives very few objections. The few that he does hear typically center on the lack of liquidity and what happens when the annuitant dies. Why? Because during an annuitant's lifetime, guaranteed income annuities have no cash value, and no liquidity. When the annuitant dies, the following things happen:

- "The cash flow from the annuity stops."

- "The principal is retained by the insurance company (but is really distributed to the other people who buy life only annuities and live)."

- "The investment is essentially lost." [53]

In order to overcome these undesired results, John explains that the life only guaranteed income annuity needs to be acquired in tandem with a guaranteed life insurance policy. The policy will insure the annuitant for the same amount, or more, as the amount they used to purchase the annuity. Thus, when they die, and the annuity disappears, the life insurance proceeds replace the money used to purchase the annuity for their heirs.

When underwriting is favorable, there will be a spread between the cash flow coming from the annuity and the cost of the life insurance. This spread doesn't always exist. But, when it does, it is as if the client has their cake and can eat it too. Often the spread is much greater than the interest that was previously earned on the assets used to fund the strategy.

In essence, then, when the strategy works, enough cash flow is generated by the annuity to both fund the life insurance premium and to more than replace the income the asset had previously generated. Equally beneficial is the fact that cash flow from the guaranteed income annuity is mostly tax-free for several years and that the life insurance proceeds are received by the client's beneficiary income

---

52 Homer, Cinderella Slipper Strategies.
53 Ibid.

tax free. If owned in an irrevocable life insurance trust (ILIT), life insurance proceeds can also go estate tax-free as well.

Example

In determining the appropriate spread, John compares the amount of annual premium that would be due on a life insurance policy with the amount of income coming in from the client's annuity. He then "matches up" the amount of annuity deposit with an appropriate amount of death benefit. For example, if a client deposits $100,000 into an annuity, that deposit could essentially be "replaced" with a $100,000 life insurance benefit when the client dies.

Annuity Payout versus Life Insurance Premiums			
Age	Annuity Payout	Life Ins Premium	Spread
60	6.20%	1.68%	4.52%
70	6.85%	2.50%	4.35%
75	8.90%	3.60%	5.30%
80	10.87%	5.20%	5.67%
85	13.43%	7.00%	6.43%
90	19.15%	10.10%	9.05%

[FROM JOHN W. HOMER, *CINDERELLA SLIPPER STRATEGIES:UTILZING THE FORGOTTEN TOOL* (2012).]

As the age of the client increases, so does the annuity payout, due to the client's shorter life expectancy. For the same reason, the amount of premium for the life insurance policy will also be higher. These factors may also create a higher percentage of spread with older clients.

The reason that the spread exists can be due to two primary factors.

First, an annuity is a present value product. This means that the insurance company receives a big lump sum from the client at the beginning of an annuity contract. But, life insurance is actually a future value product. The insurance company providing the death benefit doesn't have to pay the big lump sum out until the insured dies—which is typically going to occur at a time in the future. Therefore, there is a natural difference between present value and future value products.

Secondly, this strategy works best when two different insurance companies are used—one for the annuity and another for the life insurance policy. Because each insurance company uses their own mortality tables, some may be more competitive with annuities while others may be more competitive with their insurance products. In fact, a number of insurance companies won't even let you purchase both products from them because the difference in these spreads can cause them to lose money on the transaction.[54]

The Guaranteed Income Plan

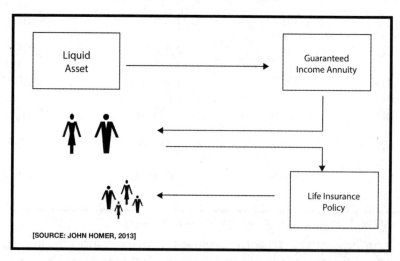

[SOURCE: JOHN HOMER, 2013]

When presenting this concept to clients, John uses the simple diagram above. It shows how the lump sum from the client converts to cash flow and how the life insurance policy creates cash for the client's beneficiaries when the client passes away.

John and his team have developed some very specific financial and estate planning strategies, purposefully for clients who are in their 70s and 80s. Some of these techniques allow clients to

---

54 Homer, Cinderella Slipper Strategies.

dramatically increase the amount of assets that will be exempt from estate taxes without causing a loss of income from those assets. He also uses other strategies with individuals and organizations, which are designed to provide guaranteed cash flow that is significantly higher than today's prevailing fixed income rates.

Case Study

John had been invited to present the strategy to the client of an accountant. The accountant had invited a colleague to come hear the presentation.

"I showed them what we had done for a lady who transferred $2.7 million of assets into a guaranteed income annuity to eliminate estate taxes on her estate. The premium for the life insurance policy was $232,000 per year.

After I finished, the prospective client turned to the accountants and asked, 'Why wouldn't I want to do this?' The second CPA, in order to show his brilliance, spoke up and said, 'Well, there is no inflation factor in this plan. You are never going to get an increase in income. You are always going to get the same amount even though your cost of living goes up over time.'

The client pointed out that the income from the bonds, in which her money was now invested, was also fixed. I then pointed out that the strategy produced 33% more spendable cash flow than her bonds are producing. I politely pointed out that the bonds are also in her taxable estate, and she stands to lose $1.5M of them to estate tax. I asked to what age this lady, now in her mid 80s, would have to live before the cash flow from an alternate investment (with inflation at 3% per year) would provide the cash flow that our plan can guarantee her today. The accountant said, 'I guess that was a rather stupid question, wasn't it.'

I then told the prospective client that I could think of several reasons why she might not want to do this plan.

1. **Whatever she puts into this plan, she can't access again.** She is trading a liquid asset that is 100% accessible to her, for a guaranteed cash flow with no access to the principal. I wouldn't advise her to consider this plan for more of her liquid assets than she is comfortable having in non-liquid form.

2. **Her plan might not be as good for her as it was in the example I had given her.** That is because I didn't know if she could even qualify for the insurance. Not everybody can qualify to get this type of strategy. For every two to three people who want the plan, only one person generally qualifies, and I didn't know if she would qualify. But then, maybe hers would be better.

What do you suppose her response was? She immediately said, 'I want to see if I can qualify. What do I have to do?' Both accountants agreed that would be a logical next step."[55]

Sometimes the client sees the benefits of the strategy being worth far more than the trade-offs, sometimes not. For advisors who are just starting to work with clients in the area of providing retirement income, John has several great pieces of advice.

One of his keys to success has been to keep the explanation of the strategy very simple. Because the strategy is for those who are ages 70-90, John always goes slowly and starts by drawing the diagram with the boxes and arrows. He does so to better illustrate the concepts of annuities and life insurance for the client. He wants to ensure that the client understands the overall concept before actual numbers are introduced into the plan.

Oftentimes, the proposal will need to be approved by the client's attorney or accountant. In these cases, John has developed a format that shows both a "before" and an "after" scenario on a single page. For clients who will have estate tax implications, John also shows the effect on the estate on the same page. This keeps everything simple.

---

55 Homer, Cinderella Slipper Strategies.

John also reiterates that in his initial presentation to clients, he does not use illustrations that are specific to that prospect. Rather, he shows these individuals what he has done for others who were in a similar situation. He tells them that their numbers will be different—perhaps better, perhaps worse. This way, clients won't be disappointed when their numbers come back differently than what they saw in the initial illustration.

When people understand what the Cinderella Slipper Strategies accomplish, the nature of the questions they ask changes from, "How much does the insurance cost?" to "How much of this can I buy?"

Advice from John

After working with the Guaranteed Income Annuity Strategy over the years, John has developed a list of tips for others who want to work in this area of the field—all of which are important to remember when presenting to clients.

- **"Think bigger, not smaller.** There is little reason to move $100,000 out of a taxable estate. But, there is usually an incentive to move $1,000,000 or $5,000,000 out of the estate. The more you remove from the estate, the more tax you eliminate. Likewise, if you are trying to increase cash flow, getting an extra few hundred dollars is not as exciting as getting an extra $10,000 or $100,000. So propose numbers that are big enough to excite people and give them a reason to want what you offer."

- **"Give your strategies names (such as the Guaranteed Income Strategy).** It helps people identify the package for what it does, not just what it is—not just an annuity and a policy."

- **"Always put the life insurance policy in force before you purchase the income annuity.** If the client dies with only one contract in place, make sure that it is the insurance policy, not the life only annuity."

- **"Do the annuity and the life insurance policy with different insurance companies.** You need to get the maximum spread. Companies have different mortality experience, and price their products accordingly. The company with the best life rates will seldom have the best annuity rates. Furthermore, some companies will not allow purchase of both products."

- **"Fund every policy generously.** Don't just fund to 'life expectancy' or age 100. If you do this enough, some of your clients will live past 100. Since there is no refund on the annuity, the family loses everything upon death if the policy is not in force." [56]

In addition, John says that there really is no such thing as a "typical" case when working with the guaranteed income annuity

---

56 Homer, Cinderella Slipper Strategies.

with life insurance strategy. However, some not-so-typical cases are certainly always welcome—especially ones like the third case that John ever wrote, earning him a $1.5 million commission. It's true that Cinderella's slipper may not fit everyone, but when the shoe fits—go with it!

**For additional information about John,
visit: www.oxfordfinancialgroup.com**

Key Points

- Income annuities are the "opposite" of life insurance.

- A team approach to planning for clients is a great way to serve their overall financial needs.

- Help clients to see their "current future" by having them take a look at non-financial issues as well as estate issues.

- The ideal clients for the Guaranteed Income Annuity with Life Insurance Strategy are between the ages of 70 and 90.

- The income annuity payout rates are actually the annual cash flow that is coming from the annuity as a percent of the amount that was used to purchase that cash flow.

- Use life insurance to "make up" for the potential loss of annuity principal—and fund the premium with income from the annuity.

- One of the keys to success for advisors using these strategies is to keep the explanation very simple.

- Don't use prospect-specific illustrations when presenting the income strategy to someone for the first time, as the actual numbers may differ.

- Give your strategies names, such as the Guaranteed Income Strategy.

- If the Cinderella slipper fits—go with it!

Retirement Income Masters: Secrets of the Pros

PART THREE

SOLUTIONS

Chapter 7:
Separating the
Truth from the Bull

"Every decision that you make is like sowing a seed, and every seed has a season and a harvest."

Curtis Cloke, CLTC®, LUTCF®
Acuity Financial / Thrive Income
Distribution System ®

Curtis Cloke
(Photo courtesy of Curtis Cloke)

Today's financially uncertain times are creating challenges for both clients and advisors. But with these challenges come the greatest opportunities for advisors to be creative and provide solutions for the difficulties facing clients. Especially gratifying are the solutions for real problems faced by honest clients who seek a path of integrity for their financial uncertainty.

For Curtis Cloke, principal of Acuity Financial in Burlington, Iowa, and founder and CEO of Thrive Income Distribution System®, LLC, creativity is all part of his success. After 26 years in the financial services industry, Curtis can certainly attest to the fact that all financial decisions are important, no matter how straightforward or creative. For this reason, Curtis is focused on providing retirement income solutions for his clients as well as providing financial professionals with retirement planning software, educational tools, and classroom training services for the distribution of retirement and estate planning solutions.

In his early days, Curtis was greatly influenced by his grandparents, and he states that the lessons he learned from them truly defined his character. One of the key principles that Curtis learned from his grandfather was to "give 10, save 10, and live on 80%." These standards were a minimum target with a goal to give more and save more over time. It was because of this that Curtis was able to purchase his first home at age 18 and soon afterward pay it off. By the time he was 19, Curtis had already purchased a $10,000 annuity, a fully funded life insurance contract, and some investment into mutual funds.

Curtis also attributes the fact that he had no debt to his grandfather's principle of "hate debt", a godsend when at age 21—married with two children—Curtis became disabled from an injury while working 630 feet underground inside a Gypsum mine and unable to work for over two years.

It was at this time in 1986 that Leon Beaty, Curtis's insurance agent and one of his primary mentors, told Curtis that he had never met anyone who made so little money yet accomplished so much financially. Leon went on to tell Curtis that he could essentially be stuck in the Social Security disability system forever...or he could "give up what seemed to be a sure thing in order to see what could be" and become an insurance agent like him.

With that in mind, Curtis spent the next year studying five top insurance companies and, on November 9, 1987, at the age of 23, he went to work for Prudential. Although Curtis is highly successful today, he did not initially start out as a shining star. In fact, he actually surprised his agency manager at Prudential by taking less of an income guarantee in order to assure he made the expected quotas, motivating himself to succeed.

For the next two years, Curtis literally hated his job

due to the repeated rejection and difficulty garnering respect as a rookie. But he had already committed to it and he was too embarrassed to fail. Plus, he had to prove the seasoned agents wrong after he overheard them taking wagers on how long he would last. That desire, combined with his persistence to succeed, allowed him to successfully close an extremely large case with the assistance of another seasoned agent and mentor, Timothy Sellner, CLU®. In 1989, they were able to close a large buy/sell agreement consisting of $10 million in life insurance with a general contracting company partially owned by a member of Curtis's church.

Something big changed in Curtis's career that day. Confidence was found through mentorship—a partnership between the experienced mentor and the less experienced mentee—creating a mindset change of "yes, I can" that became a win-win for the agents and clients involved. This set off a chain reaction of unimagined success, making Curtis the financial professional of choice selected by four of the five business owners for personal retirement and estate planning needs. This general contracting company is now in their third generation of owners and Curtis continues to have success fulfilling their needs as the financial professional of choice.

Although he began as a life insurance agent, he says that it was really the increasing needs of his clients that stretched him to expand his knowledgebase and provide broader services. Between 1992 and 1999, Curtis worked with his clients in the areas of insurance, investments, Medicare supplement insurance, and retirement planning. He found his real calling in 1999 after he discovered and pioneered the early use of the deferred income annuity for retirement income strategies for his clients.

In 1999, Curtis was a financial professional with three primary focuses:

- Life insurance for individual and estate planning needs

- Retirement income planning

- Business insurance services

Looking to expand his retirement income services, Curtis was always seeking the best methods, products, and solutions for his clients. He continues to soak up all he can and thinks of retirement as REFIREMENT! The idea of REFIREMENT comes into play during the preparation stage for retirement where much of the client's decision is emotional. Retirement is not just a financial event. To be fully prepared and mentally ready, a client should define a special purpose or mission that the retiree can focus on and be passionate about. This should motivate them, after retirement, to get out of bed every morning. Many retirees can initially experience depression after retirement because they may feel a loss of identity, less important, or no longer needed. REFIREMENT defines a retiree with purpose. Someone who remains fully engaged in life, finding fulfillment. Someone who continues to contribute to their community, church, or family.

When engineering retirement plans, Curtis fully embraces all asset classes and investment types when considering suitable product allocation options. In 1999, Curtis coined the phrase "Buy Income and Invest the Difference®." Prior to 1999, in his quest to provide the most optimal solutions, single premium immediate annuities (SPIAs) became a key staple in developing "first-phase" income as part of these retirement plans.

One day in early 1999, Curtis "accidentally" discovered a deferred income annuity (DIA) and quickly realized the power that these products can deliver secure income for retirement income planning. The actuary who first explained the contract to Curtis defined it as essentially a "delayed single premium immediate annuity." This seemed like an oxymoron—"delayed and immediate" in the same description. So Curtis would later coin this product simply as a "deferred income annuity," or DIA. Not until after 2004 would other manufacturers launch DIA products. By 2006, DIAs became more prominent, and by 2011, they became more widely developed and accepted by the industry. Eventually, Curtis's coined definition of DIA stuck as the accepted industry definition.

At a 2010 retirement industry conference sponsored by LIMRA, LOMA, and the Society of Actuaries, Curtis, accompanied by his actuary partner along with Financial Independence Group COO Brian Williams, defined the deferred income annuity while describing a "period certain" DIA ladder approach.

"A deferred income annuity, or DIA, is a newer type of annuity that is essentially a cross between a single premium immediate annuity and a single premium deferred annuity… [It] 'retains full value of the income assets for the heirs, because the designated payments are guaranteed."[57]

When engineering a retirement plan, SPIAs, DIAs, and GLWB (guaranteed lifetime withdrawal benefit) riders in combination with all other asset classes can provide clients with unparalleled secure income solutions. Essentially, Curtis figured out how to wall off a specified sum of assets to buy income. This could provide income now or in the future by utilizing a laddered income approach and then "invest the difference" for growth, liquidity, and legacy planning.

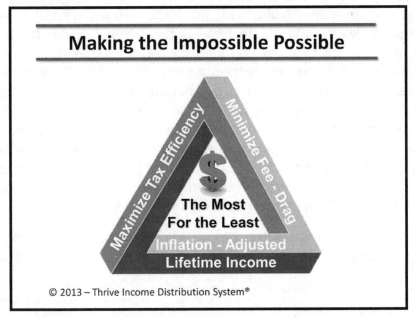

© 2013 – Thrive Income Distribution System®

---

57 Curtis Cloke quoted in Linda Koco, "What Is a Deferred Income Annuity?" National Underwriter Life & Health Magazine, April 29, 2010, http://www.lifehealthpro.com/2010/04/29/what-is-a-deferred-income-annuity.

Income annuities create three efficiencies that other product solutions can't:

- "Allow for guaranteed lifetime inflation-adjusted income"

- "Create tax efficiency through tax-exclusion ratio, aka FIBO (First In/Blend Out)®"

- "Eliminate fee-drag for assets used to generate income" [58]

When using this laddered strategy, the client initially invests a lump sum into a DIA and then delays the payout for more than 12 months.[59] In some cases, clients may elect to withhold their distributions for up to 20 years (contracts may allow up to a 40-year deferral with certain age limitations). In other words, DIAs allow you to buy income well into the future, unlike buying income now with the use of a SPIA.

The design of the DIA provides both a conventional period of delay much like the deferred annuity, where "period certain" contracts actually accumulate income value and life-contingent contracts accumulate "implied income value" that is used for asset growth, which may beat the historical baseline of traditional investment approaches. Curtis says these secure income strategies in many cases can provide "Alpha with no Beta." These payout periods are much like an immediate fixed annuity that is used for future income. The DIA product provides its owner a great combination of benefits—including protection against fluctuating interest rates, sequence of returns risk, and protection from market volatility in the years immediately before or after retirement. It offers a more tax-efficient way to take distributions from non-qualified assets, as compared to a conventional deferred annuity—last-in, first-out versus first-in, blend out (LIFO vs. FIBO℠). Plus, it has generally higher payout rates based on the sum initially allocated, compared to other types of traditional retirement income vehicles.

Curtis's discovery of the DIA was in large part responsible for his development of the Thrive Income Distribution System® and

58 Curtis Cloke, Thrive Income Distribution System®, 2011, http://www.thriveincome.com/.
59 Warren S. Hersch, "DIAs: Planting Their Roots in Fertile Soil for Growth," National Underwriter Life & Health Magazine in LifeHealthPro, August 1, 2012, http://www.lifehealthpro.com/2012/08/01/dias-planting-their-roots-in-fertile-soil-for-grow.

Thrive University. [60] Agents, Advisors, retirement income and estate planning experts, retirement academics, insurance industry experts, and actuaries are flocking to Curtis's Thrive University workshops: a two-day, extreme retirement income classroom experience in locations around the country—including private events—to help educate financial professionals who are hungry to learn more about these cutting-edge concepts and strategies. Thrive University [61] showcases its revolutionary system which may provide a contractually secure solution for inflation-adjusted income with a goal of using the least amount possible of a client's portfolio value. This creates more assets for growth opportunity or the freedom to purchase additional life insurance to secure desired legacy goals. [62]

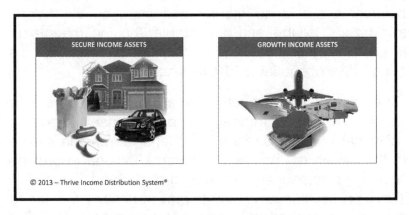

© 2013 – Thrive Income Distribution System®

The Thrive[SM] system uses an advanced algorithm that uses the power of simple income annuities (SPIAs and DIAs) in an efficient manner. The algorithm is designed to deliver a reliable income stream—regardless of what the market does—guaranteed.[63] By using only part of a client's portfolio assets for income, the remaining assets are left free to grow using traditional strategies during retirement for additional needs or to meet the client's legacy goals.[64]

60 Curtis Cloke, Thrive University: Survive or Thrive, 2013, www.thriveu.net.
61 Curtis Cloke, Thrive University: www.thriveu.net.
62 Curtis Cloke, "Curtis Cloke – Annuity, Life Insurance, Retirement Speaker," CurtisCloke.com, 2013, http://www.curtiscloke.com/about.html.
63 Subject to claims-paying ability of carrier.
64 Robert Klein, "The Thrive Income Distribution System® – A Revolutionary Retirement Income Planning System," Retirement Income Visions™, December 28, 2009, http://www.retirementincomevisions.com/retirement-income-visions/2009/12/the-thrive-income-distribution-system-a-revolutionary-retirement-income-planning-system.html.

Example

One of the key strategies behind the Thrive[SM] system is the "Divide and Conquer" method. The process first divides client assets into two categories—secure income and growth assets.

The secure income assets are dedicated for "essential" or "standard lifestyle" living expenses that the client can predetermine. The secure income provides the "paycheck"—the "value of assets needed to create a stream of annually increasing retirement income with precision." [65] Assets walled off are considered "defensive" because there is no market exposure, so the risk is minimized. Reliable and predictable, this income stream is also fully reserved by the issuing insurance carrier as a contractual obligation of the reserved assets.

Other assets that are left over are used for growth or to provide extra income for discretionary needs—a "playcheck." This stream is "offensive" as the "value of the assets not needed for income is used to provide liquidity, discretionary income, growth, and legacy." [66] These particular assets may or may not have exposure to the market, depending upon the desires and the comfort level of the specific client. Therefore, in some cases, there could be some volatility with these assets—a managed level of risk.

By separating a client's portfolio into secure and growth assets, each part of the portfolio will be positioned more efficiently in order to deliver well for multiple objectives of either sustainable income or growth for legacy, as opposed to trying to manage multiple and conflicting goals with one diversified portfolio. [67]

Curtis uses many of the same DIA income strategies that he uses

---

65 Curtis Cloke, "The Thrive Income Distribution System®," 2013 (PowerPoint presentation).
66 Ibid.
67 Ibid.

with his clients in his own personal financial situation. Another one of his grandparents' sayings was to "practice what you preach" and that is exactly what he does.

One strategy that Curtis has personally used is a "laddered" deferred income annuity technique. At age 45, he utilized "period-certain" DIA contracts to set up a series of five 5-year ladders, starting with a 20-year deferral and a 5-year payout. Each ladder would extend the delay to another 5-year period all the way to age 85, creating five designated income ladders of 5-year period certain payouts. This essentially removes all market risk, protects the targeted assets from the Danger Zone (defined as the five years before and after retirement), and provides both principle protection and "Alpha" growth (Alpha with no Beta), which would be fully realized by the portfolio whether he was "dead or alive." In this case, some internal rates of return (IRR) were competitive when compared to traditional investment approaches, some IRRs were in excess of 7% and 21% tax-exclusion ratios (FIBO[SM]) and no ongoing "fee-drag". A joint-life DIA longevity income tail completes this laddered approach at age 85, which eliminates the longevity risk and takes advantage of mortality credits for the risk of living too long. Please note, period certain DIA ladders may not be as efficient during extremely low interest rate periods as utilizing life-contingent (joint-life contingent) SPIA and DIA contracts.

Period-certain only DIA ladders do not protect the annuity buyer from longevity risk. While it can protect the return of both principal and interest growth back to the portfolio "dead or alive," it provides no mortality credits. A longevity insurance tail is an option that can be placed at the end of your last "period-certain" ladder to ensure that you will never outlive the income. Period-certain ladders in combination with a longevity insurance tail eliminate longevity risk. It wagers a much smaller portion of the premium allocation utilized to secure income assets for the longevity tail while protecting a significant portion of the premium allocation (principal and growth) to be retained by the portfolio in the event of early death. Adding an "installment or cash refund" option to the longevity tail would also protect a guaranteed principal return[68] for this portion of premium allocation but would add to the allocation requirement.

68 Subject to claims-paying ability of carrier.

Obviously, the more guarantees you place on the annuities, the higher the premium and the greater sum of total assets you will use to provide the "secure income" approach. You must balance the goals and fears of living too long and dying too soon for each client when deciding what balance of product mix is appropriate in each case.

Curtis anticipates exponential growth in DIA sales over the next 5 to 10 years. DIA sales in 2013 are projected to grow well above $1 billion, according to industry experts. [69] In his practice alone, income annuity revenue is up between 30% and 40% — due in large part to the greater acceptance of this type of product than in past years. Clients love the benefits of the secure income guarantees for their future income stream[70] when utilizing DIAs.[71]

Example

Jack and Jill, ages 63 and 62, are high-net-worth clients who wish to retire in three years. The couple has a total of $1,174,963 in joint, non-qualified assets, $76,288 in Jill's IRA, and a combined $679,496 in Jack's IRA, 401(k), and 457 plans. Their years of saving have now given Jack and Jill a total of $1,930,747 in retirement assets.

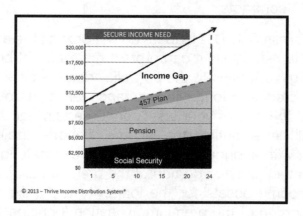

© 2013 – Thrive Income Distribution System®

---

69 "LIMRA: Deferred Income Annuity Sales Reach $1 Billion; Fixed Indexed Annuity Sales Hit Record High in 2012," LIMRA: News Releases, February 21, 2012, http://www.limra.com/Posts/PR/News_Releases/LIMRA_De-ferred_Income_Annuity_Seles_Reach_$1_Billion_Fixed_Indexed_Annuity_Sales_Hit_Record_High_in_2012.aspx.
70 Subject to claims-paying ability of carrier.
71 Warren S. Hersch, "DIAs: Planting Their Roots in Fertile Soil for Growth."

Initially, the couple's income sources at retirement would consist of monthly combined Social Security benefits of $3,158 ($2,099 from Jack and $1,059 from Jill) along with $1,425 from Jack's 457 plan and another $4,858 from Jill's pension—giving them a combined retirement income total of $9,441 per month.

Yet, based on their future projected retirement expenses and factoring in 3% inflation, the couple will actually have a projected future income gap of $11,285 per month over time.

By taking just over $422,000 of Jack and Jill's retirement assets, Curtis was able to insure enough for their "secure income assets," covering Jack and Jill's current standard of living expenses such as utility payments, food, and medication, as well as all other expenses that defined their lifestyle. In this case, the client chose to secure their "current standard" of living needs, not just their essential, with a "paycheck."

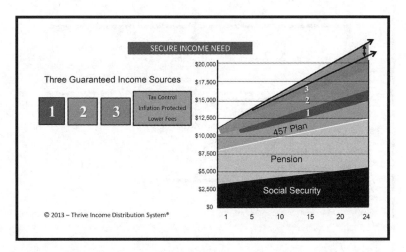

Using the remaining $1,508,448, Curtis was also able to provide Jack and Jill with extra growth in their portfolio, along with additional "playcheck" income that could be used for the couple's non-discretionary expenses in retirement.

In this particular case, Curtis was able to create three additional income sources that would "fill in" this gap. By investing these income sources in tandem, his bucket strategy allowed Jack and Jill to meet their standard of living expenses while at the same time providing the couple an additional playcheck for expenses that were considered more as "wants" than as "needs."

On top of filling the future income gap, the couple was able to obtain tax savings and meet their IRA required minimum distribution requirements. With a projective portfolio assuming a tax-deferred growth rate of 5%, they were also able to boost the potential value of their portfolio to nearly $4 million in 27 years (based on the couple's three remaining years until retirement, plus an additional 24 years in retirement).

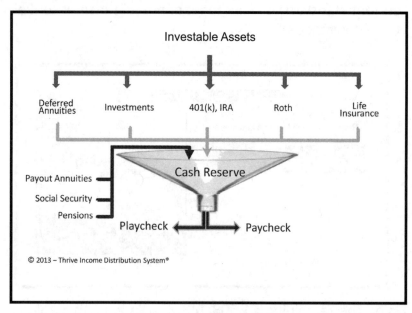

By hedging against longevity risk and market risk in addition to providing them with a legacy plan, Curtis was able to provide Jack and Jill with the financial and emotional stability that they needed for a secure and happy retirement.

The Thrive Income Distribution System® is a process-driven approach. The system takes all potential sources of a client's assets that can be used to create a number of different income streams in order to backfill the inflation-adjusted income gap. These income streams work in conjunction with other incoming cash flows, such as Social Security and pension income, in order to insure the proper amount that is needed for the client's "essential" or "standard of living" expenses. Any remaining income may then be used for more discretionary expenses such as travel, recreation, and large, unplanned purchases.

Curtis has a real specialty in cutting-edge retirement income case construction, retirement income software tools, and educational training for financial professionals in the United States and Canada. He has a way of showing financial professionals methods for optimizing their clients' retirement solutions and how to provide an efficient "glidepath" of product allocation, utilizing both traditional investments in concert with specialized income annuities in order to fill the income gaps left after Social Security and pension income is applied.

The glidepath is about matching retirement risks to the appropriate available products that address both the specific risks and concerns. It provides the income and growth goals that create emotional freedom necessary to help retirees retire with confidence.

A nationally recognized author, speaker, and motivator for the financial industry since 1999, Curtis was honored by *Senior Market Advisor* magazine as a top five finalist for "Advisor of the Year" in 2009. The American College has even tapped into Curtis's expertise to provide classroom lectures and curriculum as part of the online training of the Retirement Income Certified Professional (RICP®) designation. He has been a 14-year MDRT member, a 3-time qualifying member of Court of the Table, and a 6-time qualifying member of Top of the Table.

I first met Curtis at a Top of the Table meeting in Kauai when I was speaking on the main platform. It was the first time that I delivered my Paychecks and Playchecks presentation. Looking back, although it was very well received, I didn't feel that it was one of my best deliveries. Curtis, however, loved every minute of it. I had barely walked off the stage and there he was, grinning from ear to ear. I could tell he was thinking, "Finally, someone is speaking my language!"

He proceeded to take out his computer and walk me through his Thrive Income Distribution System®. He was talking about DIAs, which I had very limited knowledge of at the time. While I found them very interesting, some of the numbers he was showing me looked too good to be true. But there they were. Somehow, I was still a little unconvinced. As a senior executive officer of a Fortune 100 company, I just felt that these products had to be mispriced. Here is the one guy, basically in the whole country, who found a pricing anomaly and was exploiting it. Besides, I told him, the DIAs he was using had no mortality credits. They did not take longevity risk off the table.

Over the next couple of years, Curtis and I stayed in touch. As I did more research, I found that he was really on to something. I think during this same period, Curtis did some research on mortality credits and found that I was on to something as well. It was then that we were really ready to see how we could work together.

We have spoken at several industry meetings together and I have had Curtis do some of my personal retirement planning. He is so meticulous—matching income with Social Security timing and tax and legacy planning. His spreadsheets are so detailed that I get a headache just looking at them.

He has developed cutting-edge software that can help any producer who really wants to become a retirement income pro. Curtis can get deep, deep in the weeds when it comes to retirement income. He knows the details better than anyone I have ever met. He believes in his process so much that he can seem overbearing at times—but anyone who really knows him knows that it is just his passion for retirement income.

He strongly believes that retirement is a time to REFIRE for things most important in your life. He counsels advisors to avoid the fleeting promises that may or may not last or take unnecessary risks when establishing the REFIREMENT income floor.

Curtis's grandmother had one more family remedy. She loved family meals and church potlucks. While cleaning up leftovers and utensils from the meal time, she would always say, "Keep your fork... the best is yet to come!" She was of course talking about dessert.

Retirement is the dessert. It can be a blessing or a curse. Curtis fondly remembers his grandmother's phrase. When applied to retirement, it can be one of the sweetest times of your life.

Advice from Curtis

Curtis knows that talk is cheap and people want to see results—which is exactly why he articulates to advisors how to generate the maximum inflation-adjusted income for clients while using the least amount of their portfolio.

By refining his approach and developing effective techniques to communicate his ideas to others, Curtis has essentially cracked the retirement income code for how to successfully position income annuities and longevity insurance to clients.

When working with clients on constructing a retirement income strategy, Curtis reminds agents that it is an absolute must to take longevity risk off the table. He states that there are three key things that an advisor must focus on: income, arbitrage (i.e., using life insurance to replace annuity deposits upon an annuitant's passing), and longevity.

Curtis never mentions specific products up front. This way, he can focus solely on comparing benefits that the client will receive, as well as on what the client can really expect in return. "It's all about 'framing,' although advisors really need to understand the math and science behind the products as well."

Curtis states, "All products are good, and all products are bad"—he is not committed to just one particular product for all clients. Yet, it is essential to first mathematically come up with a certain amount of necessary income as a "floor," while also adjusting for inflation.

As Curtis learned early in life from his grandfather, each decision in life is like sowing a seed. Each seed has a season and a harvest. And when the harvest comes, you reap what you sow, more than you sow and in the measure in which you sow.

Curtis compels financial professionals to know and understand the math and science behind the products they sell. As professionals, we are sowing seeds for our clients' futures; the harvest will come, and our clients will reap the harvest of the seeds we help them sow. So sow well!

**For additional information on Curtis,
visit www.thriveu.net**

Key Points

- Make use of objective, defined processes and systems.

- Help clients to interactively participate in planning their retirement income strategies.

- Link clients' expenses to specific income-producing sources and assets.

- Combine the use of interactive technology with specific processes to customize a retirement income plan for clients.

- Help clients to ensure that they will never outlive their money.

- Financial planning is not just an event; it is truly an ongoing process.

- Become process-driven versus product-centered.

- Stop talking at clients, and focus more on working with them.

Chapter 8:
Ensuring Safe Withdrawal Rates Aren't "Too Risky" nor "Too Safe"

"My passion is to help advance the financial planning body of knowledge and distill complexity into practical applications that advisors can use to create better solutions for their clients." [72]

Michael Kitces
(Photo courtesy of Michael Kitces)

Michael Kitces, MSFS®, MTAX®, CFP®, CLU®, ChFC®, RHU®, REBC®, CASL®
Pinnacle Advisory Group, Inc. / The Kitces Report

Determining just how much can be safely spent in retirement has been a hot topic for several years. This debate is largely due to the financial service industry's substantial focus on retirement income, coupled with the oncoming wave of retiring baby boomers. The use of safe withdrawal rates on client assets has increased in popularity in recent years, even as criticism of this "overly mechanistic" approach has grown in the post-2008 low-return environment.[73]

Nonetheless, when trying to determine a reasonable floor to a client's retirement income, the safe withdrawal rate approach can provide a great deal of value for those who wish to determine a starting point for the standard of living that a particular asset base can sustain. Michael Kitces, MSFS, MTAX, CFP®, CLU®, ChFC®, RHU®, REBC®, CASL®, of Pinnacle Advisory Group, believes that financial advisors can learn a great deal from research to lead them

---

72 "About Michael," Kitces.com, 2011, http://www.kitces.com/about.php.
73 Michael Kitces, "Resolving the Paradox - Is the Safe Withdrawal Rate Sometimes Too Safe?" The Kitces Report, May 2008, http://www.kitces.com/assets/pdfs/Kitces_Report_May_2008.pdf.

to better fit the right income-producing vehicles and strategies to specific client scenarios.

Through his skillful contributions to the firms in which he has worked, Michael has realized that there is an opportunity to leverage his passion even further to truly advance the financial planning body of knowledge and the quality of solutions that financial planners deliver to their clients. While his day job is director of research for Pinnacle Advisory Group in Columbia, Maryland, it is likely that most people know Michael from his prolific writing on the art and science of financial planning in his newsletter, The Kitces Report, and his popular industry blog, Nerd's Eye View. InvestmentNews recently recognized his contributions and lauded him as "one of the premier thought leaders in the financial advice industry." [74] As one of the original founders of NexGen, Michael proves his knowledge and capability through the array of financial planning designations that he holds.

> As his interests have always been diverse, Michael has mastered the art of balancing his time between many pursuits. The child of two computer scientists, he graduated from college with a split focus on psychology, pre-med, and theatre. Upon graduation, he came to realize that he did not want a career in any of these fields.

> Not sure what to do, Michael took a job at New England Life, where he spent the first few years selling life insurance. It wasn't until he developed a focus on more comprehensive financial planning—with a concentration on the emerging products and strategies to craft retirement income recommendations—that he really found his calling.

Over the years, Michael has had working experience in many forms of financial planning—a traditional commission-based model, a blended fee-and-commission practice, and a research-based role for the fee-only firm in which he currently works. This diverse background has given Michael a broad perspective on the difficulties

74 Jason Kephart, "15 Transformational Advisers: Michael Kitces," InvestmentNews, June 18, 2013, http://www.investmentnews.com/article/20130618/FREE/130619891#.

that financial planners face—especially with regard to the challenge of staying up to date in an ever more complex world of systematic withdrawal strategies, annuity products, and more.

When using the safe withdrawal rate for creating retirement income, the first step is to determine a rate of withdrawal that will allow the client to comfortably meet their regular living expenses. This rate—and its corresponding dollar figure—are determined up front, at the time of initial retirement. This amount will also act as the "income floor," even if market returns force a change in rate over time. Applying the safe withdrawal rate contrasts with previous methods of creating retirement income that simply moved assets into income-producing vehicles over a 30-year period.

The problem with this prior approach to creating retirement income is that even if markets average 10% and 5% respectively (or 7% and 2% of real returns once 3% inflation is factored in), markets can still undergo significant periods of time with varying returns. For instance, the real returns of balanced portfolios have ranged from under 3% to over 8% for a decade or more. And, compounded over a long-term timeframe such as 30 years, a range of 3% can add up to a significant amount of money over time.

As a result, the goal of the safe withdrawal rate approach was simple—set the initial spending level low enough that even if a bad sequence occurs, the withdrawals can be sustained for 30 years, giving time for markets to rebound.[75]

---

75 Michael Kitces, "Resolving the Paradox."

Example

Using a portfolio of $500,000 with a withdrawal rate of 4.5%, a retiree could essentially withdraw $22,500 in the first year of retirement with Social Security, pensions, and any other fixed retirement income sources to supplement. If adjusted for a 3% rate of inflation, the retiree would withdraw $23,175 in year two. However, due to market movements that can affect the portfolio balance, the actual withdrawal rate percentage will vary to some extent in later years; nonetheless, the goal of the approach is to maintain that $23,175—with additional inflation adjustments in the future—regardless of market returns. By having set the withdrawal rate low enough, the portfolio can survive even unfavorable bear markets and temporarily higher withdrawal percentages. [76]

Michael is well known throughout the financial services industry for his ability to make the difficult easy. But somehow, of all of the people featured in this book, I may know him the least. In our interview for this book, we jabbed a little back and forth—I clearly lean toward the use of lifetime income annuities, Michael leans more toward withdrawing from a diversified portfolio. Though, he remains open to the use of annuities in many client-specific situations.

The research is extensive on both sides. Certainly, in most cases, a withdrawal rate may indeed work. However, I feel that if there is even a 10% or 20% failure rate, you won't feel any better if you are the one whose plan fails. Yet, Michael points out that the failure rate of the strategy for the past century has been 0.0%.

I recommended to Michael covering basic expenses with guaranteed lifetime income and then optimizing the rest of the portfolio to protect against inflation. Michael immediately countered that almost none of his clients see the world in "basic expenses" and "discretionary expenses." Rather, they just need a number to live their life by. Or alternatively, if it is important to set an income floor expected to last for life, the safe withdrawal rate is intended to be a floor that lasts for 30 years and has never historically failed over

---

76 Michael Kitces, "Resolving the Paradox."

any 30-year time horizon.

Despite his reasoned approach, I still believe that you must take longevity risk off the table. Stocks, bonds, mutual funds, and managed money just cannot do it. When I asked him, "What happens if medical technology increases life expectancy to 100, 120, or 150 years of age," Michael reminded me that most of the increase in life expectancy has been due to reduced infant mortality. There is no promise of a lifetime beyond 120 years yet (which he points out has always been the maximum human life span even as we've increased the average life expectancy along the way). In addition, Michael notes that if longevity unexpectedly improves dramatically, at least a few annuity companies will have serious financial risk as well. In other words, he says it's not entirely clear whether it's safer to bet on which annuity company will survive unexpected population longevity or to just maintain control of the portfolio and make your own adjustments as life and medical advances occur.

As you can infer, we had a stimulating conversation. I wanted to include Michael in the book because there are advisors who still swear by the withdrawal rate method. While I may not practice it myself, I can respect it.

Michael admittedly does little in the area of lifetime annuitization in his current practice. However, he has been heavily involved with such products under several different firms and business models over the years—and he has spent a great deal of time on research in this area as well. In fact, it was the subject of his first book, *The Advisor's Guide to Annuities.*

Michael recognizes that immediate annuities can be a powerful tool to hedge longevity risk, especially for clients who rank that as their greatest concern and are willing to give up flexibility and upside to manage that risk. Michael especially likes the concept of longevity insurance—essentially a DIA where a client aged 60 to 65 puts 10–15% of their portfolio into a DIA that will begin paying guaranteed lifetime income at age 85. With a DIA, the advisor only needs to plan for income for a fixed period of 20 or 25 years; this significantly simplifies the portfolio construction and planning challenges. The caveat Michael notes, though, is that the burden is still on the advisor to correctly "guess" what inflation will be for the next 20–25 years, or risk under or over-allocating money to the DIA, although future product enhancements may help to resolve this concern.

I would add that this is how I see most investment-oriented advisors getting comfortable with guaranteed lifetime income. As I said in *Paychecks and Playchecks*, this puts all of the mortality credits at the end of your life. Meaning, the advisor can still retain significant assets under management and the client is guaranteed income for life by a process completely backed by math and science — an all-around win!

One income-related product that has fallen out of favor with Michael over the past several years is the variable annuity (VA). Until recently, he was a big fan of them; however, as the cost of VAs has risen, these products are becoming less of an option for Michael's clients. As the general cost of risk has forced pricing higher and expected returns have dropped, it's simply difficult to beat the guaranteed rates, and Michael notes that if the goal is just to get a guaranteed rate, immediate annuities and their mortality credits offer the better deal now.

Certainly, the greatest fear of retirees is of outliving their money. According to Michael, only slightly less worrisome than this is the risk that retirees will live so long that inflation erodes their wealth and income so much that they are unable to maintain their current standard of living.

Yet, if income annuities can offer a solution to inflation and the lifetime income dilemma, why is it that some clients still object to these products? Michael feels that there are a variety of potential reasons — starting with the fact that advisors may not always do the best job of explaining how income annuities work and the benefit that they can provide.

Another fear that may be keeping clients from placing large sums of cash into annuities is the legacy factor. In other words, while such financial vehicles do answer the longevity issue with lifetime income, in many cases the deposited funds disappear when the client passes away. In addition, there's also the simple challenge that when funds are already liquid, clients have a hard time giving up that liquidity. In any case, Michael feels that a big part of client objections comes from irrationalities.[77]

Example

> Michael suggests imagining a proposed retirement income solution for a client as follows: "Every paycheck during your working years, we're going to take a portion of your income, and allocate it directly to a future retirement annuity. You can't touch the money when it's paid, or at any point thereafter, even if you desperately need it for a dire emergency. Your retirement contribution to the future annuity is mandatory, and it will be a non-trivial portion of your paycheck (e.g., 6%). You can only start the annuity payments when the annuity company says you have reached a reasonable retirement age. If you're married, the annuity payments will be made on a survivorship basis, but if you pass away without a spouse—or are the second to die of the couple—no future payments are made. All of your remaining savings in the retirement annuity are gone. If you're single, you can save (and will, since it's mandatory!) in the retirement annuity for 40 years but if you pass away right before retirement, all of the money is gone and you can't bequeath any of it; the annuity company keeps it." [78]

For many people, this retirement savings and income scenario would not be appealing at all. It forces people to save, yet it prevents them from touching the funds until a certain time. It also prevents them from leaving a legacy for their heirs, does not offer any flexibility, and forces a multi-decade deferral period before payments can begin.

Yet, many people are already very familiar with this type of "annuity"—it's referred to as the Social Security program. In most cases, it is viewed as being a fundamental pillar of one's retirement

---

77 Michael Kitces, "If Immediate Annuities Are Such a Great Solution, Why Doesn't Anyone Want to Buy One?" Nerd's Eye View, February 2, 2011, http://www.kitces.com/blog/archives/112-If-Immediate-Annuities-Are-Such-A-Great-Solution,-Why-Doesnt-Anyone-Want-To-Buy-One.html.
78 Ibid.

income.

The bottom line is that our views about retirement income solutions vary drastically depending on how they are presented. This is especially true in light of how such solutions can work for particular client situations, while at the same time allowing for as little downside as possible.

Advice from Michael

When it comes to providing advice for advisors, Michael has a strong belief that given the difficult market environment, advisors may be in danger of experiencing the "three strikes and you're out" risk over the near term. Meaning, there is a real possibility that if clients have to go through a third bear market in just over a decade, advisors may begin to really start losing clients.

"Advisors and their clients 'weathered the storm from 2000 to 2002' and then another [bear market] from 2008 to 2009. But there comes a point where clients just start to capitulate," Kitces says.[79]

What will really help advisors gain appeal with their clients is by using more active products and strategies to manage risk. In addition, advisors need to connect with clients more effectively; one way to do this is to take advantage of the digital age and the technology that is emerging. Much of this technology will impact everything that financial advisors do—for instance, by making financial planning a much more engaging and interactive process that helps clients get the buy-in they need to stick to their plans.

The wide reach of the Internet will also allow clients to seek out and work with advisors who more closely match their individual needs, regardless of the geographic area in which the client and the advisor reside. As a result, it will become more important than ever to clearly have a niche—in retirement income, or other areas— because generalists will just find their clients slowly picked off by an emerging range of specialists.

Certainly the biggest factor when working with older clients is for advisors to manage the uncertainties and risks that they face. How can this be done? First, it is essential to plan conservatively for the long-term time horizon, if not outright hedging exposure to longevity risk. In addition, it is imperative for advisors to do their homework and keep up on the latest research as it adapts, to ensure the right solutions are applied for each individual client situation.

Michael also states that there is a lot of research that is lacking

---

79 "Michael Kitces: The 2012 IA 25 Extended Profile," Think Advisor, May 9, 2012, http://www.thinkadvisor. com/2012/05/09/michael-kitces-the-2012-ia-25-extended-profile?ref=desktoplink.

for many of the income-producing products available today. This can quickly lead to confusion. Advisors must understand the entire range of products and solutions that exist—as well as why or why not to use them with particular clients.

One way to really get up to speed on product information and planning methods is to participate in structured, formal financial education. Michael suggests one of the best ways to accomplish this is to obtain one or more of the financial services professional designations that are available. Start with the Certified Financial Planner (CFP®) that is offered through organizations like the College for Financial Planning, the American College, and local educational institutions across the country. Then go beyond the CFP® certification to obtain advanced knowledge and specialization to truly differentiate yourself from others. With this knowledge, you will be able to ensure that the client's retirement income solutions—whichever path you follow—won't be too risky nor too safe.

For additional information on Michael Kitces,
visit www.kitces.com

Key Points

• The financial services industry has shifted to having a substantial focus on retirement income over the past several years.

• The safe withdrawal rate approach can provide a great deal of value for those who wish to determine a starting floor for the standard of living that a particular asset base can sustain.

• It's not enough to just use historical rates for returns and inflation to craft retirement (and insurance) recommendations; as the safe withdrawal rate research has shown, it's better to plan around the potential worst-case scenarios, not merely the averages.

• DIAs are valuable—especially once their income has begun—primarily due to their ability to hedge clients' longevity risk.

• Oftentimes people's perception of how retirement income works can be irrational, even though those perceptions can dominate the decision-making process.

• How solutions are presented is a key factor in getting clients to buy into the solution—particularly when recommendations are adapted to work for clients' specific situations.

• Over the near term, some advisors may face the "three strikes and you're out" risk, given the difficult market environment.

• What can really help an advisor to gain appeal is by using more proactive strategies and products to manage risk and by advancing their knowledge and education to remain competitive.

Chapter 9: Solutions for the Uncertainty of Retirement Income Needs

Richard P. Austin
(Photo courtesy of Richard Austin)

"Everyone thinks running out of money is about the day that you run out—when in fact, it is really about the years prior to that when you know you are going to run out of money. You just don't know when."

Richard P. Austin, CLU®, ChFC®, CRC®
Consultant to the Financial Services Industry

Lifetime income annuities can be the perfect solution for many retirees: these annuity payout income streams never run dry. They quiet the fear of running out of money. In addition, by supplementing income with annuities, more of a retiree's portfolio is allowed to grow, giving it the chance to last longer. With lifetime income annuities, retirees can obtain income for their spending needs, as well as receive help in fulfilling their bequest desires.[80]

Richard "Dick" Austin, CLU®, ChFC®, CRC®, consultant to the financial services industry in the areas of marketing, business development, and retirement planning, stresses the reality that investment planning doesn't end at retirement. In many ways, the true reason behind all your years of saving is just beginning—the future is here. The retirement nest egg that so many people work to build is the means by which they will be able to enjoy retirement in the way that they had hoped.[81]

---

80 "A New Beginning," Ibbotson Associates, 2003.
81 Ibid.

Originally from Chicago, Dick attended Bradley University knowing that he wanted to work in the business marketing field. After four years in an Air Force Intelligence Unit during the post–Korean War period, Dick finally settled in Miami, Florida, to begin his career in 1961.

He developed his marketing, sales management, and product development skills during his 26 years with The Travelers Insurance Company. He was recognized for his accomplishments as he served as vice president of market development at First Financial Planner Services, a subsidiary of The Travelers Corporation.

With his expansive experience in the business, Dick has realized that the challenge today is retirement's "extended unemployment." Retirement can now last longer than a retiree's actual working and saving years, spanning 20 years or more. This longer-than-projected retirement can create some real challenges as it relates to keeping assets protected and to producing lasting retirement income.[82]

There are three risks that arise from this longer life and retirement. They are:

• **Market Risk** – Market risk is actually a concern for investors even before retirement, although it continues during retirement as well. Most people remember the market panic and sleepless nights of 2008 and 2009, when the Dow lost approximately 50% of its value seemingly overnight. Savings that took years to build were literally decimated, leaving many who were retired or quickly approaching retirement having to drastically alter their plans. Market risk can be a huge concern for retirees, as it could mean the difference between continuing a comfortable lifestyle or going back to work in order to "make up" the lost income.

• **Inflation Risk** – Those who are living on a fixed income will also run into inflation risk—the fact that purchasing power will decrease over time. The value of a retiree's income has the possibility to decrease as inflation shrinks the purchasing power of their income.

---

82 Richard P. Austin, "IVAs Respond to Consumer Longevity Concerns," LifeHealthPro, January 15, 1996, http://www.lifehealthpro.com/1996/01/15/ivas-respond-to-consumer-longevity-concerns.

For example, given just a 3% rate of inflation, a retiree's income of $3,000 per month today would need to be closer to roughly $4,700 per month in 15 years in order to buy the very same products and services. But remember, there may also be periods of time when inflation can be much higher than 3%. And, even with the historically low interest rate environment we've been living in for the past several years, it can be difficult at best for retirees who are living on a fixed income to keep up.

• **Longevity Risk** – Today, people are living longer than ever before. In fact, it is estimated that the average 65-year-old male will now live to 86, while the average 65-year-old female will live to age 89. Yet, once again, these are just averages. While one person may die much younger, another could live to the ripe old age of 100 or more! The bottom line is that, by the very nature of people living longer, their retirement assets and income will also need to be stretched out over many more years—and in conjunction with all the other risks like inflation and market volatility. This essentially means that longevity can actually magnify, or multiply, all the other risks.

As discussed in *Paychecks and Playchecks*, longevity is not just a risk—it is a risk multiplier of all the other risks in retirement. If you retire at age 65 and drop dead at age 68, it doesn't matter if the market drops 4,000 points. It doesn't matter if you were withdrawing 10% per year from your portfolio. It doesn't matter if you forgot to buy a long-term care policy. You didn't live long enough for these to matter! However, if you live to age 80, 85, even 90—all of those other risks could wipe you out.[83]

The traditional solution to the longevity issue, then, called for a larger beginning portfolio balance, lower spending during retirement, or the use of financial products with a higher amount of investment risk. These solutions often fell short.

In addition to these primary risks, many retirees not only want to have enough money for themselves, but they also want to leave a legacy—to family, to charity, or to both. With this in mind, the more that the retiree spends in income during retirement means less money available for these wishes.

---

83 For more information about retirement risks, consult Chapter 2 in my first book, *Paychecks and Playchecks: Retirement Solutions for Life* (Acanthus Publishing, 2012).

Example

Take a 65-year-old couple who has a total of $1 million at retirement, with 50% of their money invested in stocks and 50% invested in bonds. After factoring in Social Security, the couple needs $50,000 in additional annual retirement income. In this case, how long will their portfolio last?

According to Ibbotson Associates, there are thousands of possible scenarios on how the market may perform in the coming years. But by taking an overall summary of the possibilities, we can generate an estimate of how long the couple's portfolio may last given their $50,000 annual income.

In roughly 50% of the cases, the portfolio will last until the couple reaches age 100. Yet, while that can provide some peace of mind, there is still a chance—albeit a slight chance—that at least one spouse will live past age 100.

If, however, the market tumbles—as we saw recently in th economic downturn of 2008 and 2009—the couple isn't so lucky with their retirement funds and will likely only be able to maintain their portfolio until they reach age 88. The chance is much greater that at least one of the spouses will be living past that age and will need the income that was being generated from the funds.

So, what are the choices that can help the couple make their assets last longer? Well, one option would be to simply spend less. Yet, for most people—and especially for those at retirement—spending less isn't always a viable option. This is especially the case should one or both spouses encounter adverse health conditions that require costly medical treatment or medications.[84]

Not only is the risk of running out of money crucial, Dick also stresses the fact that asset allocation for retirement income must deal with return volatility risk. Oftentimes consumers and advisors confuse asset allocation with product allocation. But there is a big

---

84 "A New Beginning," Ibbotson Associates, 2003.

difference between the two, which he defines as:

• Asset Allocation: "the decision of how to diversify between different asset classes like stocks and bonds, [which] is an important decision that helps you to manage financial market risk"

• Product Allocation: "the decision of how much of one's portfolio to keep in a particular product category such as mutual funds, stocks, bonds, or annuities" [85]

As mentioned, both consumers and financial advisors underestimate the number of years that they will spend in retirement. One of the most common mistakes that investors make is ignoring the financial and longevity risks in retirement by using withdrawal rates that are based on average annual investment returns and the anticipation of living no longer than the "average" life expectancy.

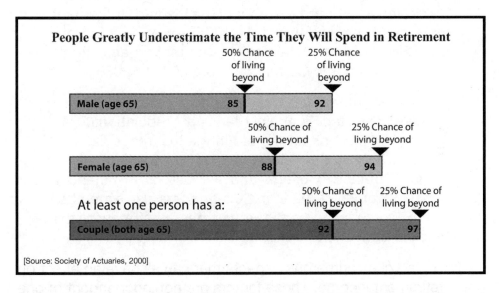

[Source: Society of Actuaries, 2000]

On average, a 65-year-old retiree with a $500,000 portfolio and a $40,000 annual income need, who believes that long-term market returns will be sustained, may feel comfortable withdrawing that amount each year. However, the likelihood of plan failure is high with a:

• "10% chance of running out of money by age 75"

85 Richard P. Austin, "Built to Suit," 2013 (unpublished article).

- "25% chance of running out of money by age 77"

- "50% chance of running out of money by age 80" [86]

Just as in the accumulation stage when a long-term growth of funds and liquidity is essential, there are also some critical decisions that a retiree must make during the decumulation stage of their financial life as well.

Dick states that people simply aren't accustomed to spending down a lump sum at retirement versus getting a regular paycheck throughout their working lives. They have a difficult time grasping this concept, so they oftentimes make unwise choices when it comes to what they should do with their retirement funds.

Dick's presentations on the subject of retirement income planning at national conferences and company seminars explain how to avoid the problems mentioned. He served as a board member of the Insured Retirement Institute (formerly NAVA), and in 2005 he was inducted into the IRI Hall of Fame. He also chaired that organization's Retirement Income Committee from 2001 to 2008.

Dick is a member of the Society of Financial Service Professionals, the Financial Planning Association (FPA), and he is a past-chairman of Florida Insurance Council (FIC). He holds a Bachelor of Arts in Social Science from Florida Southern College and a Master's in Financial Services from the American College. He is also a member of the Executive Committee and past-chairman of the Pinellas Education Foundation.

Dick also cites numerous aspects that can all have an effect on one's retirement income. These factors are not independent of one another, so each may either influence or be influenced by another. These factors include:

• **Age** – "As age increases, annuitization becomes more beneficial and allocations will generally tend to increase."

• **Health Status** – "How retirees feel about their health, relative to

---

86 "Retirement Income Planning," Ibbotson Associates, 2002 (PowerPoint presentation).

their peers. Retirees with above-average health may have a longer-than-average retirement and therefore annuitize a greater portion of their portfolio. Annuitization becomes less beneficial for retirees with below-average health and a shorter expected retirement."

• **Bequest Desire** – "The balance between retiree income needs and desire to leave money to heirs will greatly influence the use of immediate annuities. Annuitization levels will be higher with a greater income need and lower with a high bequest desire."

• **Annuitization Preference** – "Retirees may prefer guaranteed income from an immediate annuity—'annuitize more.' Other retirees may find the benefits of annuitization are outweighed by the costs and/or risks—'annuitize less.' Some retirees use annuities to cover only essential living expenses and use other income sources for discretionary expenses. As it makes sense to diversify investments—'don't put all your eggs in one basket'—it also makes sense to diversify sources of income during retirement."

• **Risk Tolerance** – "Measures the ability to handle investment fluctuation and the possibility of loss. It influences the asset allocation of a portfolio and indirectly influences how much to annuitize. There is a risk of loss associated with buying an annuity. Payouts on annuitization products are based on average life expectancy. A person who lives past average life expectancy earns a return; and a person who dies before average life expectancy experiences a loss." [87]

• **Product Choice** (i.e., annuities versus non-annuitized investments) – While all situations will be different, the choice of financial products that one chooses will have a great deal to do with factors such as age, risk tolerance, income need, and desires to pass something on to heirs.

• **Sequence of Returns** – While average returns may be important during the accumulation phase, it is the order, or sequence, of returns that become most important once your portfolio becomes your primary income generator. In fact, once you begin taking money out of a portfolio, average returns really don't matter at all. Sequence of returns essentially refers to the fact that if you face a market decline

87 Richard P. Austin, "Built to Suit."

in the years just before or just after retirement, it can have a drastic impact on your retirement income. This is because you no longer have time to "average" out a better return; rather, you are left with the amount of money that you have following the decline. It is from this lesser amount of funds that your retirement income will now be based.

As it relates to the time that will be spent in retirement, retirees should plan to live to age 100. This is especially the case when working with couples because at least one of the spouses is likely to live to—or beyond—that age.

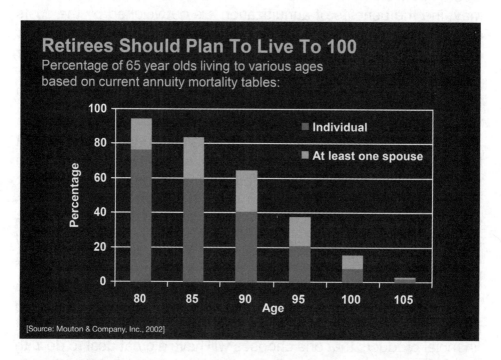

So what is a retiree supposed to do to reduce longevity risk and optimize their income? They must use some form of guaranteed lifetime income—usually a lifetime income annuity from an insurance company. Study after study proves that annuities are the most efficient and effective form of optimizing and guaranteeing income for life.

Prior to 1986, retirement income product choices did not usually include annuities. After the Tax Reform Act of 1986, that changed.

A key reason for the change was that the 1986 law eliminated or reduced tax deductions in hugely popular real estate, oil and gas, and other programs, structured as limited partnerships. However, the valuable benefit of tax deferral on investment gains continued for deferred annuities. For that same reason, distribution of annuities widened as banks, broker dealers, and financial planners all began offering these products.[88]

> Around that same time in 1987, Dick and two colleagues quite literally started an insurance company from scratch, offering immediate annuities as a group insurance product. He served as the president of Templeton Funds Annuity Company, the life insurance subsidiary of Franklin Resources, from 1987 until 2002. In that role, Dick had an overall responsibility for the development and distribution of Templeton annuity and insurance products.
>
> In addition, between 1998 and 2000, Dick was deputy chairman of Templeton American General Life of Bermuda, Inc. He was responsible for sales and marketing of offshore life and annuity products. Then, from 2002 to 2006, he was retained by Ibbotson Associates to provide consulting services in business development and marketing. Dick has served as marketing consultant to Toronto-based annuity service provider CANNEX Financial Exchanges Limited. He is periodically engaged as an expert witness in FINRA arbitration cases relating to insurance and annuities.

Over the years, Dick realized that the message being projected to boomer and pre-retiree investors has changed. Accumulation has shifted to decumulation, or the spend down of the assets that have been gathered throughout one's working life.

But Dick has found that the use of annuities can help to relieve the pressure on portfolios. Annuities can provide income while at the same time offering growth and asset protection, which is especially beneficial in a poorly performing market. In addition, these products

88 Richard P. Austin, "Training Financial Advisors: The Key to the Evolution of Annuities," 2004 (PowerPoint presentation).

can help manage financial risk by wrapping several asset classes in a long-term diversified portfolio. It is also possible to provide a "hedge" against longevity risk by using lifetime income annuities, as these products literally pay their holders an income for the remainder of their lives. This tends to take longevity risk off the table entirely because income will continue regardless of how long the recipient lives.

When comparing this type of certainty to more "traditional" spend-down plans, it can really highlight the weaknesses—and the risks—of these types of retirement income plans.

Example

Dick tells a story of a group of Northeasterners who had always wanted to visit the desert:

"They romanticized about seeing sand dunes, lizards, and a cactus or two. So they fly to Death Valley, California, get a rental car, and head across the desert, through Nevada and into Arizona. The temperature is over 120 degrees but they are enjoying the air conditioned comfort of their large Lincoln Continental.

The day is beautiful and, as their car moves through the acres of giant Saguaro cactus, the occupants of the vehicle chatter about the wonderful scenery, the nice, warm sunshine, and the great time that is being had by all.

After a while, the occupants notice a road sign—Next Gas Station 100 miles. Someone notices that the tank is rapidly approaching 'E.' Now the mood of the passengers changes. No longer does the scenery matter. The previously 'nice, warm sunshine' becomes uncomfortably hot as the occupants turn off the car's A/C and roll down the windows in the hope of saving fuel. The remainder of the trip is spent with a constant fixation on the fuel gauge. Arguments begin about how fast they should drive and what they will do when they run out of gas in the middle of the desert."

Running out of money is just like running out of fuel. Everyone thinks it is about the day that you run out. But it is really about the years prior to that. You *know* that you are going to, you just don't know when. Just like the glaring red "E," many people in retirement are just staring at their "gas gauge"—their brokerage or savings account balance—waiting for it to run out. It is about the loss of peace of mind in retirement and the inability to enjoy the "scenery" along the way.

Using lifetime income annuities can remove the constant fear of running out of money—providing retirees with financial peace of mind, a reduction in stress, and a much larger quality of life overall.

When explaining the value of annuities to clients, it is always best to keep things simple. In a nutshell, the mechanism of annuity payouts is really quite basic. What they provide is a flow of dollars that combines the return of the investment (i.e., the principal) with the return on the investment and some extra dollars from the risk pool (i.e., the investment return and mortality credits).

When comparing the use of a lifetime income annuity with other potential income-producing options, the following can be useful:

> "If a withdrawal from a regular investment account is made each year that is exactly equal to the payment received from an annuity with the same initial value and investments, the value of the investment account would decline to zero at the retiree's life expectancy."[89]

However, because annuities are insurance contracts, all participant investments are pooled and the contributions of those who die before their average life expectancy are applied to those who continue to live past their average life expectancy. This is a concept that is referred to as mortality credits.

What exactly are mortality credits? In essence, they are a financial "reward" that increases the longer you live. Therefore, the more years you spend holding a lifetime income annuity, the more mortality credits you will be paid. They are based on actuarial calculations by the insurance company that issues the annuity that

89 Richard P. Austin, "Living Too Long with Too Little Money: A 'New Era' for Retirement Planning Payout Annuities – Myths and Realities," Journal of Retirement Planning, May–June 2002.

are based on your age and gender, and they add a credit from the entire risk pool of everyone who buys the same type of lifetime income annuity. When doling out mortality credits, because some of the people who buy lifetime income annuities will die earlier than expected and will therefore not collect as much—if any—annuity income, the insurance company can pay the remainder of those in the pool a bit more. This often represents a higher "return" than many of the other types of traditional income-producing investments that are purchased by retirees.

Annuity contracts are also backed by a guarantee from the issuing insurance company, stating that if their mortality calculations prove to be incorrect and the average life expectancy of the participant pool is longer than originally projected, resulting in a cash-flow shortfall, the insurance company will make up the difference—a factor that is not seen with any other type of investment. This, then, places the risk of making good on their promise directly on the shoulders of the insurance company, not on the investment itself. This is also why insurance companies are required to carry a certain amount of reserves in order to make good on such guarantees.

Annuities are a form of insurance, and they share an important quality with all other forms of insurance. People do not buy insurance products because they offer the potential for the greatest financial gain; they buy insurance products to offset the risk for great financial loss. Running out of money in the later stages of retirement is a great financial loss, which can be prevented with a lifetime income annuity. The ultimate benefit of insurance, in any form, is peace of mind.

Advice from Dick

For those of you who are contemplating moving into the retiree market, Dick has several great pieces of advice.

Begin by having a thorough understanding of the challenges that are now being faced in retirement. The biggest of which include:

- Stretching retirement assets to last much longer than in the past

- Aggregating and converting assets into a lifetime income stream

- Rejecting a "one-size-fits-all" solution to retirement income management

Therefore, it is best to work with a retirement income management process that consists of assessing retirees' needs, identifying income resources and gaps, identifying and managing retirement risks, identifying distribution and estate issues and opportunities, converting resources into income, and maintaining and updating the plan as needed.

Certainly, it goes without saying that advisors should learn everything they possibly can about lifetime income annuities. In addition, one of the best ways to obtain clients who are in need of income strategies is to partner with a rep who is nearing retirement and then work with that rep's clients who are also approaching the retirement phase of their lives.

For additional information on Richard Austin,
visit http://www.planningtampabay.org/net/frmPeoBio.aspx?id=6661
or http://www.zoominfo.com/p/Richard-Austin/1881574

Key Points

- Lifetime income annuity payout streams never run dry.

- Investment planning does not end at retirement.

- The three key risks that are faced by retirees are market risk, inflation risk, and longevity risk.

- Retirees who wish to leave something behind will need to take less income for their retirement living expenses.

- As it relates to the time that will be spent in retirement, in most cases, retirees should plan to live to age 100.

- The message to boomers and pre-retiree investors has changed from accumulation to decumulation.

- The use of annuities can help to relieve the pressure on portfolios. They can provide income, and at the same time offer growth and asset protection.

- The volatility of returns combined with the unpredictability of life expectancy makes more traditional spend-down plans far too risky for many retirees.

- In addition to financial issues, constant worry about finances can also wreak havoc on the quality of a retiree's life.

- Advisors should learn everything they possibly can about lifetime income annuities

Bob Hartman
(Photo courtesy of Bob Hartman)

Chapter 10: Designing the Ideal Income Solution

"My goal is to help my clients select the best combination of products and services to meet their objectives while delivering an unparalleled level of personalized service to each client."

Bob Hartman, CLU®, ChFC®, CASL®
New York Life

Oftentimes, people put off planning for the future simply because they don't understand the basic concepts. They don't know how plans should be developed and implemented, so they wait. This lack of understanding may be part of the reason that less than 50% of all US workers have actually determined how much money they will need to save for a comfortable retirement.[90]

After 41 years with New York Life, Bob Hartman, CLU®, ChFC®, CASL®, knows how much of a difference educating his clients can make. Bob is really a one man band. Although he occasionally partners with other agents and takes full advantage of New York Life's product consultants and General Office resources, he doesn't even have an assistant or a secretary. Based in Carefree, Arizona, he provides a portfolio of insurance and other financial products that assist businesses and individuals in their planning efforts.

Yet, he does more than just plan. He believes that in today's

90 "2012 RCS Fact Sheet #4: Age Comparisons Among Workers," Employee Benefit Research Institute and Matthew Greenwald & Associates, 2012, www.ebri.org/pdf/surveys/rcs/2012/fs-04-rcs-12-fs4-age.pdf.

world, "excellence" is no longer good enough. He seeks to provide "world class" service. One of the key reasons for Bob's tremendous success as one of the company's top lifetime income annuity producers nationwide is his personal experience in knowing how lives can change in an instant—and how different things can be for those who plan ahead.

> Bob's father was a factory worker who passed away when Bob was 12 years old. After losing the household's breadwinner, his mother took a job as a clerk in a department store. At the age of 12, Bob learned the value of responsibility and the importance of helping out both yourself and your family. To lend a hand, he got his first job as a plumber's assistant at that time.

> Luckily, Bob's uncles stepped in and became great mentors to him after his father passed away. He learned a responsible work ethic which carried over into his college years. Between his freshman and sophomore year, Bob decided that he did not want to go back to school without a car. As his mom didn't have any money to help him, Bob worked two jobs for the whole three months of the summer—and returned to school in the fall with a car, an old MGB. He still remembers how great it felt paying for that car on his own.

Knowing how connected people are to their hard-earned money, Bob seeks to provide the soundest way to help clients preserve their wealth. To educate his clients and prospects, Bob provides in-depth information and financial calculators directly on his website. Just some of the questions that these help to answer include:

- "How much retirement income will you need?"
- "Should you refinance your mortgage?"
- "How much life insurance is enough?"
- "What type of IRA is right for you?" [91]

While these calculators aren't intended to predict future results

91 "Calculators," New York Life, 2013, www.bobhartman.com/calculators.cfm.

or act as a substitute for sitting down with an actual professional advisor, they do help site visitors get an approximate assessment. By briefly answering these common financial questions, Bob's website helps turn prospects into clients.

Case Study

Bob's client was a retired—and very wealthy—businessman. Up until that time, the client had been relying on traditional tax-free fixed income investments for his retirement income. He had a maturing $100,000 CD and simply wanted some ideas from Bob on what to do with the money.

After Bob described the features of the lifetime income annuity, the client decided to purchase a onetime fixed annuity with the $100,000. At this time, the client also said it was very unlikely that he would ever add any more money into an income annuity.

However, after some experience with his annuity, coupled with the declining income from his traditional fixed income investments, the client contacted Bob and placed some significant additional funds into the plan.

As of this writing, this client is receiving an attractive income, of which a very small percentage is taxable. This case study really highlights the tax advantages of the exclusion ratio for non-qualified lifetime income annuities.

In the summer of 2011, the client stipulated via trust that his 16 beneficiaries must purchase lifetime income annuities with their inheritance—and these annuities must be purchased through Bob Hartman or his successor agent. The client wanted to help his heirs but didn't want to ruin their lives by giving them large blocks of money. He preferred that they receive guaranteed income for the rest of their lives.

During this time, deferred income annuities became very popular in the industry. So in early 2012, Bob wrote a deferred income annuity on each of the beneficiaries. The client has since added additional funds to each, as he and his spouse are entitled to add up to $26,000 annually and still qualify for the annual gift exclusion.

Going forward, the client plans to add additional funds each year into each of the deferred income policies. Upon the client's death, what is left of this trust will also be divided into each of these 16 deferred income annuities. Quite a change from his initial hesitation over the income annuity concept!

Bob credits such success with guaranteed lifetime income strategies to the Paychecks and Playchecks mentality. He is truly a student of the industry, as he was always the first to show up and last to leave whenever I spoke at New York Life training meetings.

Although Bob was offered a partial baseball scholarship to Penn State University, he attended Thiel College in Greenville, Pennsylvania, where he received his Bachelor of Arts in Business in 1969. Even though Bob has some regrets about not attending Penn State, he was able to participate in both the baseball and wrestling teams at Thiel.

After graduating in 1969, Bob took a job at Ernst & Ernst, and then, after only a year, he moved on to GE Financial. In all, Bob had three different jobs during the first three years out of school. At that time, his uncle—one of Bob's mentors—sat him down and said that he needed to "decide what you're going to do with your life. You've been out of college three years and have had three jobs—if you keep this up, no one is going to hire you." His uncle's candid advice really resonated with Bob, and he has been an agent with New York Life for over 40 years!

An early adopter of new ideas, Bob found that he especially liked the lifetime income annuities and deferred lifetime income annuities because they fit his marketplace so well.

Case Study

In early 2011, a 80-year-old Holocaust survivor contacted Bob. He was worried that some of the reparation payments that he was receiving would end at his death. He wanted to ensure that his wife would have adequate income for the rest of her life as well. He decided to purchase a lifetime income annuity that would provide her income for the rest of her life.

About six months later, the client came back to Bob to purchase another lifetime income annuity that would provide him and his wife additional income for the rest of both their lives. The lifetime income annuities had given them the confidence and peace of mind that they had been looking for.

While many financial and insurance professionals talk regularly with clients about how they would like to leave a legacy, they will also work to be remembered by their clients and their clients' loved ones. Bob Hartman is no exception.

In 1972, after thinking over what he wanted to do with his life, Bob went to work for New York Life Insurance Company in Erie, Pennsylvania. At that time, the company basically only offered whole life, term life, and major medical insurance. But as the company has grown, Bob's business has grown along with it, continuously offering customized strategies for the varying needs of his more than 800 clients—the majority of whom are in the pre- and post-retirement stage of life. He has served on numerous boards, including the Society of Financial Service Professionals, Greater Phoenix Chapter, and he is a past-president of the Carefree/Cave Creek Chamber of Commerce.

Bob strives to do the best possible job in assisting his clients to plan for securing retirement income. That includes making sure that their money does what they want it to do.

To accomplish this, Bob now uses a combination of both deferred income and guaranteed lifetime income strategies. He uses the lifetime income annuity for immediate income and the deferred income annuity to give additional income in the future to help with inflation or other additional income needs in retirement. The lifetime income annuity is an alternative that many seniors find attractive for their traditional IRA accounts. At age 70 ½, they must begin taking required minimum distributions (RMDs). The income from the lifetime income annuity satisfies the RMD requirements. It also gives the clients stable, predictable income for the rest of their lives. He states that the lifetime income annuity has really been a very good solution for roughly 70% to 80% of his clients. Bob has even used the deferred income annuity as a college planning tool since parents (often pre-retirees) can set the income start right when they will need it for college expense and then use it for their own retirement once they no longer have educational expenses.

Prior to using guaranteed lifetime income strategies with his clients, Bob was a big proponent of using variable annuities and mutual funds to address many of his clients' needs. But today, in light of recent market conditions, putting too many assets into the market can represent too much of a risk for many of his clients. And while mutual funds may be good accumulation products for many clients, they are not necessarily good vehicles for guaranteed income needs, due to the fact that both principle and interest fluctuates with market conditions.

Case Study

Bob wrote his first lifetime income annuity in the middle of 2006. His client, who was in his early 80s, had all his money invested in the stock market. Although the client was comfortable with his money being there, Bob explained that he was taking a very big risk: If there was ever a market correction, the client would likely not recover.

Bob helped his client see that his current situation might not be prudent given his age, so instead the client purchased a lifetime income annuity. In doing so, Bob was able to provide the client with guaranteed income to cover his living expenses—a "paycheck." With the remaining funds that the client kept in the market, he was able to also obtain funds for an additional playcheck. In the years that followed, the client was particularly thankful for Bob's help and guidance. Their relationship continues and the client recently purchased a second lifetime income annuity for legacy purposes!

Over time, Bob has used lifetime income annuities with RMDs, even if the client is not currently in need of income. The increased cash flow can allow them to give more money to children and charity while they are alive. It can also be used for life insurance or long-term care premiums to further leverage those dollars. Clients also really like using lifetime income annuities with the "stretch IRA" technique because it can often set up a guaranteed fixed income stream for their heirs. To do this, set up joint lifetime income annuities with the client and each child or grandchild. Not only will the client get a fixed stream of income for life, but also each child or grandchild will also get a fixed stream of income for the rest of their lives as well.

Yet, as beneficial as the use of this strategy can be for many individuals, very few beneficiaries ever actually set up the "inherited IRA." Bob has recognized this fact, so he helps the client understand the pros and cons; many clients then set them up before they die. Bob brings up the lifetime income annuity as an alternative with many of his clients as it can help lock in a certain amount of regular fixed income. And, as long as clients can cover their basic living expenses with this income, it frees up the remainder of their money for other goals and expenses.

Case Study

Although Bob no longer spends a lot of time marketing through cold sources, he still runs a newspaper advertisement in his local paper. This ad has generated a number of calls through the years, which have resulted in some nice business. One particular case involved a person interested in receiving a stable check each month of about $1,000. After learning more about the client's financial situation, Bob felt a lifetime income annuity might serve the client well. The client asked to think about it for awhile. Meanwhile, Bob left for a planned vacation. While Bob was out of town, the client decided he wanted to move forward with the annuity. Not able to reach Bob, the client called another financial advisor, saying he wanted to buy an annuity that paid $1,000 per month. The other advisor, not knowing he could solve for a monthly amount, said he needed to know how much the client wanted to invest before he could quote a monthly amount. Frustrated by the lack of understanding by the other advisor, the client decided to wait for Bob to return from vacation to get exactly what he wanted.

The approach that Bob uses to discuss income strategies with clients comes down to asking the client two basic questions, and then, based on the client's answers, proposing solutions and options to address them. These questions include:

- "What do you need your money to do?"

- "What do you want your money to do?"

Bob will sometimes get feedback from some of his clients related to the fact that they would be sacrificing potential growth and liquidity. In most cases, the problem can be solved by explaining in more detail how the product works—and to consider not placing 100% of one's funds into the annuity. Once clients realize that they will have a base income with which to cover expenses and the remainder of the funds still available for other things, they are then ready to move forward. In many instances, clients have come back and asked to add more lifetime income annuities to their overall financial plan.

As far as alternatives to lifetime income annuities, there may not be too many, depending on the individual client's specific situation, needs, and time horizon.

Because life insurance and financial products are rarely bought spontaneously, agents must help the client understand the reasons why they need them. To do this, Bob makes a point of participating in ongoing educational training. He frequently attends meetings and webinars, and he has attained a number of designations from the American College. All of this additional training gives him the tools to assist his clients in creating their "financial blueprint" and, of course, makes sure he always has an in-depth understanding of clients' needs. Bob gives some tips to how agents can develop this understanding:

• **"Review your individual situation and personal objectives."** Because every individual and family situation is unique, it is essential to find out as much as possible about their financial goals. The more that is learned about a client, the more precise recommendations can be made.

• **"Analyze and review your needs."** Bob works with clients in identifying and prioritizing objectives and then establishing benchmark goals. Because there are so many choices today, people typically try to accomplish too much at once—or they don't attach specific deadlines to their goals. By helping clients to break down their goals into specific objectives and time horizons, clients are better able to look at the resources they have available and then decide which of their goals are realistic, which ones need to be adjusted or scaled down, or which ones should simply be abandoned.

• **"Develop and implement a strategy to help you achieve your goals."** Based on client conversations and analysis, Bob can recommend the insurance and financial products that can help clients meet their goals.

• **"Coordinate your financial activities."** In addition to coordinating products, Bob also helps clients coordinate their plans with other advisors as well, such as their CPA and attorney. This way, everyone is "on the same page" in terms of moving forward with the client's specific plan.

• **"Monitor progress; provide ongoing service as your needs and situations change over time."** Because financial planning is not just a one-shot deal, strategies will need to periodically be adjusted as clients' lives change. Therefore, clients' financial plans are regularly reviewed and tracked—and changes are made as needed. [92]

---

92 Bob Hartman, "My Services," New York Life, 2013, www.bobhartman.com/My-Services.3.htm.

In moving through this process, nothing is ever assumed. The client's plan is based upon thorough and regular communication. Bob encourages clients to ask lots of questions of him, especially for more details and explanations about the recommendations that have been made and about how certain plans may work. Bob also stresses to clients that it's never too late to start planning for retirement and finding a source of guaranteed fixed income.

Even though Bob makes recommendations that are based on client goals and objectives, all decisions in terms of actually moving forward with a plan are in the hands of the client. With this in mind, the client must ultimately be comfortable with the outcome.

By asking clients questions, Bob is able to custom fit income solutions to his clients' exact needs. In doing so, clients can almost sell themselves on the right plan. With the client happy, Bob is too.

Advice from Bob

For insurance and financial professionals or advisors who are considering using lifetime income annuities as alternatives for their clients, Bob offers two key pieces of advice. First, connect with an experienced advisor who is already working in this market and pick their brain or even sit in on some of their appointments. This experience will help you define the types of questions and concerns that can arise. It will better inform you and put you in a position to address some of these concerns with your own clients, which should help you build confidence. Second, read *Paychecks and Playchecks*: "It is a compilation of many different strategies and possible fixed income solutions and alternatives."

The truth is, though, that experience comes in visualizing your success and then going out and actually doing the things that will make you a success. Overcoming objections, for example, is really just a matter of helping the client to better understand the product or strategy. In moving through objections, it is also good to ask additional questions of the client. This will help to ensure that all sides of the objection have been addressed.

In other instances, it may be a question of simply tweaking your recommendation to make a client feel more comfortable. For instance, if a client is concerned about having liquidity when they purchase a lifetime annuity, then overcome this objection by putting a smaller portion of their assets into the annuity.

**For more information about Bob Hartman and his strategies for providing lifetime retirement income, visit:
www.bobhartman.com**

This section represents a general overview of how Robert Hartman started his career in financial services and how certain principals, training and experience have helped him to be effective in the area of retirement income planning. Robert Hartman is not affiliated with the author, Tom Hegna. Nothing in this Chapter is to be considered an offer of any specific product or service, nor is it intended to provide any specific tax advice. Readers are advised to consult a professional focused in the areas discussed to help them address their specific situation.

Key Points

- Our lives can change in an instant—so it's best to be financially prepared.

- Lifetime income annuities can be an excellent solution for many clients who are in need of regular fixed guaranteed income.

- Lifetime income annuities can be used in numerous strategies, including college planning and providing retirees with stable and predictable income.

- Clients need a "paycheck" to cover their basic expenses; they can use the remainder of their funds to obtain "playchecks."

- Ask clients two key questions: "What do you need your money to do?" and "What do you want your money to do?"

- Educating clients on retirement income strategies, solutions, and alternatives can help to ease some of their concerns about growth and liquidity.

- By asking clients questions, the advisor is often led directly to the plan of action that is best for their client.

- Ask questions of more experienced advisors in order to learn all you can about lifetime income annuities and how they can fit into various client situations.

Retirement Income Masters: Secrets of the Pros

PART FOUR

THE ROLE OF THE ADVISOR

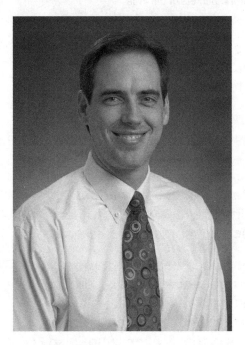

Dave Christy
(Photo courtesy of Dave Christy)

Chapter 11: Retaining Clients Is the Number One Key to Growth

"Agents and advisors can truly 'insulate' their business by offering additional products to their existing clients."

Dave Christy
National Property & Casualty Agency

The more of your products that people own, the less likely they are to move their business to another company. With this in mind, any professional or business owner knows that it's much easier to keep existing clients than it is to bring in new ones. When it comes to offering lifetime income strategies, property, and casualty, insurance agents can have a real advantage—starting with the trust that they've built with their existing clients. In many cases, these clients lead to several generations who want the same care and attention that their parents received. They may even be the recipients of the agents' care and are already appreciative and ready for their guidance.

Dave Christy, a top producer for a Fortune 100 property and casualty company, is a firm believer in offering clients a variety of financial and insurance tools to help them in multiple areas of their lives. He knows that the more products a client owns, the more likely they will stay with you. Adding lifetime products like life insurance, long-term care insurance, and lifetime income annuities multiplies the effect. In fact, Dave has never lost one lifetime income annuity client in 15 years—these products can really bind clients to your agency. In this regard, retirement products like the ones he has used can be considered a strong client-retention tool.

Dave learned just how important protection products can be when his father passed away while Dave was in college at Washington State University. Thanks to the proceeds from a life insurance policy, Dave and his two sisters were able to finish their education without his mother needing to struggle financially. It was his father's careful planning that left a lasting impression on Dave.

A talented baseball player, Dave had high hopes of making it to the big leagues one day. While that dream did not come true, he did stay active in sports, playing in several men's leagues for fun. In one such league, he played basketball with a stockbroker who also sponsored the team. His expensive home and significant income intrigued Dave. He wanted to know more about what the stockbroker did and what he should do with his own money, specifically his life insurance money, and his mother's.

Seeing his drive and determination, the broker offered Dave a job after he graduated from college. Once in the financial industry, Dave studied even more about the concepts of wealth. He began cold calling in order to obtain clients and found that he really loved the financial services business.

Curious about whether financial advisors themselves invest in products other than those offered to clients, Dave asked his boss one day, "What do financial reps buy for their investments—what's the good stuff?" His boss's response was not what Dave had expected: "Products really don't matter that much until you truly understand your clients' needs."

His boss' sagacious response has stayed with Dave and taught him the importance of planning for specific clients. Even though

Dave loved the equities business, in 1994 he moved over to a major property and casualty insurance company, feeling that the P&C arena was more stable. Since that time, his business has grown exponentially, and he currently has 12 experienced team members to help clients with any questions or concerns that they may have. Having a diverse and knowledgeable staff allows Dave to continue his passion of working directly with his more than 4,000 clients.

Dave credits one of the biggest components of his agency's growth to Shirley Retherford. Their unlikely partnership began one day when Dave went into his local bank. He noticed a middle-aged woman named Shirley who was always busy meeting with bank clients. Everyone wanted to talk to her about their finances because she "made it seem easy." One day near closing time, Dave noticed that Shirley was available. Quickly seeking her assistance for a routine banking matter, he began to notice all the plaques and awards on her wall. Not only was she a top producer in the banking industry, but she was also a top annuity seller. Dave has since learned a great deal from her experience and expertise.

When Dave's company entered the banking arena, it seemed the only plausible step was to bring Shirley on board. She knew banking; and with Dave's background in equities, they made a great team. But it was really their clients who benefited on all angles.

In fact, Dave and Shirley often debate how people should best retire. Laughingly, Dave recalls that in the beginning, clients would "politely decline" his market-related options and then purchase an immediate annuity from Shirley.

"Shirley has a way of relieving clients' stress about having enough income in retirement. Because of this, there was room for both of us and our views in the agency." Since that time, Dave says he has essentially "backed into" the annuity market and now has a niche market of primarily senior women.

Given the positive aspects of bringing Shirley into the agency, Dave has continued to hire where his weaknesses are. By pinpointing the gaps in his business, he can focus on his own strengths and have staff experts in other areas to create the most dynamic offering possible. Clients are able to be matched to the team member who can help them the most. Altogether, this makes Dave's agency the obvious choice for customers.

Dave believes that P&C agents have a gold mine of potential income annuity clients sitting right in their own agencies. Although P&C agents generally work with an entire spectrum of clients, not all clients have the financial resources for retirement income products or extensive financial planning. Although Dave works to help everyone better their situation, he has trained his staff to seek out clients with the resources that require more complex needs. He especially seeks clients who are in need of retirement income.

The young family just starting out or the newly licensed 16-year-old driver, for instance, is not going to be a candidate for lifetime income strategies. In other cases, even if some clients love the concept of lifetime income planning, they may not have the assets or disposable income. There is, however, a percentage of clients who will be an ideal fit for lifetime income annuity strategies—and it is these people who are likely to remain clients for life if they are able to gain peace of mind through an income they can't outlive.

Even if a client does seem to be an ideal fit, Dave still hears objections. The most often heard is the "irrevocable" decision. Some lifetime income annuity clients have a hard time grasping the concept of parting with a large sum of money, even if those funds will be returned in the form of guaranteed and lasting income for however long they may live. With help from Paychecks and Playchecks concepts, Dave explains to clients that liquidity is not a one-time event—it is a lifetime event. Adding some guaranteed income to a portfolio increases lifetime liquidity. And by using a portion of the portfolio for guaranteed lifetime income, clients gain control over key retirement risks—like longevity risk, order of return risk, market risk, and withdrawal rate risk.

One of the alternatives that Dave has used with some of his income clients is the laddering strategy. Dave purchases multiple annuities over a period of several years. This way, clients are able to increase their income over time with each additional income stream that is added. By putting smaller sums of money into several different annuities with differing start dates, Dave also eases clients' concerns about parting with a large percentage of their overall assets all at one time.

Case Study

In one particular instance, a friend of Dave's—a retired property and casualty agent—asked if Dave would take over his family's insurance policies. Honored to do so, Dave soon discovered that the family had many insurance policies.

Not long after retiring, the friend was diagnosed with leukemia. He told Dave that there was no one else in the world whom he trusted more with his money. So he asked Dave to help his wife with finances upon his passing. Dave of course obliged.

One caveat, though, was that the agent's wife was extremely risk adverse and did not like the volatility of the equities market. She became stressed if she didn't have money in her bank account to provide her with a financial cushion.

Reviewing the policies that the agent had transferred over, Dave noticed quite a bit of life insurance and various investments. The one product that the agent did not have was an income-producing annuity.

As the agent's illness rapidly progressed, Dave had numerous conversations with him. Dave described how he would be able to "create a regular paycheck" for the agent's wife from the life insurance proceeds after he passed.

Relieved that his wife would be taken care of financially, he asked Dave what type of product could create such an income stream. In all of his years in the insurance business, the older agent had not become familiar with annuities and how they work. Thanks to Dave's recommendation, the husband could be at peace knowing that the wife would be in a good financial position for the remainder of her life.

With many success stories like this one, Dave is a valued member of the industry. He now sits on the Insurance Department Advisory Board and is a member of the National Association of Insurance & Financial Advisors. I first met him in 2011, when he heard me give my Paychecks and Playchecks presentation. While retirement income was not a new concept to Dave—his office had already been doing many of things I talk about—he now knew that he had "math and science" on his side.

Advice from Dave

As an agent with a bent toward the P&C market, Dave's advice to those wishing to pursue lifetime income strategies with clients is to first and foremost let people know that you can help them in other areas of their financial lives as well. Agents can easily increase sales—and retain clients—by simply showing clients other areas where the agent can help. One of the biggest advantages that property and casualty agents have, according to Dave, is the ability to meet with clients on a regular basis. You have their individual and undivided attention, so the property and casualty insurance products you already offer can create a "springboard" to other product sales.

Annual reviews, for instance, are a perfect time to bring up the fact that you represent other product lines. Of course, be sure that you truly understand all the tools in your toolbox before all else. In bringing up other product lines, like income annuities, keep the conversation light. Talk to them about the possibility of not needing to work during their retirement years.

In any case, it's good to have a process in place for offering these products. You've already got the relationship with most clients, giving you the added advantage of pre-existing trust. In Dave's case, he typically sees roughly two-thirds of his 4,000-plus clients at least once every other year.

Dave has also found that talking to seniors about income annuities can be an ideal win-win situation. Most seniors have the time to meet with you—and they will listen if you have viable strategies. This group also typically has the available funds to invest. They will be trusting of you—as long as you're sincere.

Once you've identified good potential annuity buyers, you should plant the seed early in the relationship. Keep in mind, though, that in most instances, these are not quick product sales like auto or home insurance. However, they are very worthwhile to both your clients and your business.

By offering income annuities and other financial products, Dave has been able to insulate his business. Offering other types of solutions to clients eliminates the price competition that has become so fierce in the home and auto insurance market today. Clients are much less likely to leave you—especially based on price alone—if you are solving multiple needs for them.

Remember, you will always add clients over time; the really good agents are the ones who also keep the clients they have. Above all else, the key to success in the property and casualty world is to not lose current clients.

**For more information on Dave,
visit www.davechristyinsurance.com.**

Key Points

• Property and casualty agents have pre-existing trust built in with their current clients.

• Offer your clients a variety of products that can help them in all areas of their lives.

• Income annuities can be a successful client-retention tool.

• Products don't matter until you truly understand your clients' needs.

• Hire where your weaknesses are. Match clients to the team member who is best suited for their needs.

• Make your agency the obvious choice for clients.

• All P&C clients may not be suited for income annuities—but the ones who are will likely remain clients for life.

• Have a system in place when bringing up additional product lines, and use annual reviews as an opportunity to discuss such products.

• Plant the seed about income annuities early in the client relationship.

• Clients are much less likely to leave you—especially based on price alone—if you are solving numerous needs for them.

Chapter 12:
It's Not About Fees—
It's About Value and
Performance

"There is so much that people don't understand about financial strategies. If they just talk to someone who knows how to plan, their lives could be so much better. My job is to eliminate fear."

Christie Mueller
New York Life / Christie Mueller & Associates

Christie Mueller
(Photo courtesy of Christie Mueller)

No one's life is perfect; we all make mistakes along the way. While some missteps could have been prevented, it is the learning from each that truly adds value. As a financial advisor, it is just as important to impart your own life lessons to clients. By showing them that you truly understand their situation because you've been there, you will create a more valuable connection, be more successful, and feel more fulfilled.

Christie Mueller, a top performing female agent at New York Life Insurance Company, has an ability to connect and listen to clients' needs and wishes. As one of the top 50 performing agents in the company, she has built a reputation for her deep knowledge of retirement accumulation and income distribution strategies. But she didn't always know that she would be a successful agent.

Leaving Iowa for a degree in English literature at the University of California, Santa Barbara, Christie worked for 10 years after graduation as a news anchor and reporter at several CBS television stations. During that time, Christie lived in Boise, Portland, and Seattle before deciding to make a midlife career change.

While not exactly sure what she wanted to do, Christie knew that her next job had to involve helping people in some way. Yet, when presented with a viable opportunity to create a difference, she almost walked away without even giving it a second thought.

It all began when Christie was attending a children's Christmas pageant. She struck up a conversation about her decision to change careers with the woman sitting next to her. The woman suggested that Christie meet with her husband, a highly successful insurance agent.

Upon hearing the word "insurance," Christie immediately closed her daytimer. She told the woman that she would pass. Christie admits that she stereotyped insurance agents as being "portly gray-haired men who all wore white suits."

As Christie moved to put her daytimer back in her purse, the woman stared at her incredulously. "I can't believe you just did that. You closed your mind without getting any information."

Rethinking her oversight, Christie opened her mind—and her daytimer—and set a meeting with a top-producing New York Life agent. And the rest is history.

But Christie's career in financial services wasn't all easy. In fact, for the first 10 years in the business, Christie readily admits that she did not like her job. She spent more time thinking about going back to her past career than she did looking ahead. "I am the poster child at New York Life for how not to do it," she quips. Even though her struggles continued for a decade, Christie persevered.

For many years, Christie knew that even though she believed in the benefits that the financial vehicles such as life insurance could provide, she just wasn't passionate about it. It didn't help that she really didn't "get" the concept of lifetime income strategies.

She didn't truly understand lifetime income until her father passed away, leaving her mother worried and scared that she didn't have enough money to survive. After running the numbers, Christie discovered that her mother would be able to live very comfortably with the income that a vehicle like lifetime income annuity could provide. While many retirees want to leave a legacy for their children, Christie told her mother to spend her money on living expenses and be comfortable.

As she was dying, Christie's mother kept asking if the money was going to last. Christie was able to say, "Everything is fine, Mom." She could see the relief in her mother's eyes. Giving her mother that peace of mind was priceless. Christie has now been able to duplicate this feeling over and over again with the many clients she has been able to help.

While she really can't nail down the exact moment when her perception about her job changed, Christie suddenly realized one day that she truly liked her clients. In return, they seemed to appreciate how she was helping them.

Case Study

Christie remembers a particular client whom she delivered an annuity death benefit check to in 2002. Throughout the whole process, the client seemed a little fidgety. She would look down at the check, back at Christie, then back to the check. Finally, the widow told Christie that the check was too much—"This is more than my account value."

Christie reassured the woman that she was fully entitled to that amount, due to the guaranteed death benefit offered by the annuity.

That amount not only took care of the client and her husband while they were both alive but continued after the husband passed away. Cases like this remind us that these types of financial "products" can help enhance the quality of clients' lives.

As with many top producers, Christie knows how important it is to "not only talk the talk, but also to walk the walk." If you can relay a personal story about how the products you sell have worked successfully in your own life, it tends to ease clients' fears about moving forward.

> At age 58, after going through a painful and costly divorce, Christie was facing the need to start over financially. She was terrified that she wouldn't have enough income in retirement. So, she decided to run an income annuity illustration for herself, starting at age 65.

> This, too, was an eye-opening moment for Christie. She realized that with the illustrated payout rate, she could have a comfortable, guaranteed fixed income for the future. Currently, many experts say that only 3.5% to 4% can be safely withdrawn from a diversified portfolio (and Morningstar recently lowered that to 2.8%). Since the annuity payment consists of principal, interest, and mortality credits, the payout rate can be higher. Even better, it is guaranteed for life by the issuing insurance company.

In her marketing for new clients, Christie focuses on large companies with groups of employees who have worked together for many years—ideally all in the 55-year-old age range. She knows that these individuals will soon be retiring and need help with transitioning their accumulated savings into an income stream. She feels that co-workers who are also long-time friends have a similar way of thinking and acting. She sees people as being "weeds or flowers"—a group of people who have worked together will typically sort out the weeds, leaving only the flowers. These flowers are among Christie's ideal clients.

Another type of client that Christie places as a high priority are those who have recently been laid off from their jobs—a group that has grown fairly substantially given the recent recessionary economy. Because qualified funds can be used in many of her retirement income strategies, Christie is able to take large 401(k) and IRA rollover money and convert it into lifetime income paychecks for her clients.

Case Study

> Christie recently met with a couple where the husband had been laid off. His goal was to find a new job, work for another four or five years, and then retire. But after running an analysis for them, Christie discovered that in order to achieve their goals, the husband would really only need to work part time for a few more years before he could comfortably retire.
>
> This discovery almost instantaneously removed the worry about the need to find another high-paying job—which was not only creating financial stress, but a strain on the marriage as well.

Christie states that transferring over large lump sums that already exist is much easier for clients to justify than starting from scratch or setting up a new plan that will require out-of-pocket funding. And, these rollover funds can also be converted to income for her clients right away, so they essentially see an immediate, positive result.

With so many con artists preying on older individuals, annuities can provide the perfect solution for reducing a large pool of assets. "Someone receiving $2,000 per month, for instance, will be much less of a target for scam artists than someone who has a half-million dollars just sitting in the bank," Christie posits.

Regarding this exact point, I quoted David Babbel and Craig Merrill in *Paychecks and Playchecks* as saying, "Sometimes we pay a very high price for maintaining what we think is control." [93] Income annuities can help protect many elderly people who, because of age or dementia, can be easily confused and taken advantage of.

---

[93] David Babbel and Craig Merrill, "Investing Your Lump Sum at Retirement," The Wharton School, University of Pennsylvania (2007).

Case Study

Christie recalls one instance where her clients, a retired couple, had plenty of money but not a lot of income. While they were able to purchase many items outright, they were unable to qualify for a home loan because they had no regular incoming cash flow.

Christie advised these clients to take a portion of their savings and convert it into a guaranteed lifetime income stream. Soon after doing so, the couple was easily able to qualify for a loan to refinance their home. In fact, the clients rave about how happy they are to receive incoming checks on a regular basis.

Because of this regular guaranteed income stream, the clients no longer need to worry about regularly rebalancing their investment accounts, either. They have additional peace of mind as their worries about future market movements have also disappeared.

The really interesting part about this case, Christie states, is that she never even thought about this couple as having a need for income. This goes to show that you really shouldn't automatically rule anyone out as a potential client for a lifetime income strategy.

Christie values educational moments like these to change her perspective as a financial advisor. Early on to supplement her learning, she decided to obtain motivational training from a company that teaches people about their cognitive abilities as well as how to effectively set and achieve goals. This additional guidance helped Christie to catapult her attitude, goals, and overall career to the success that she has gained today.

Every year since 1997, Christie has qualified for New York Life Chairman's Council, which is based on yearly production. And, each year since 2001, she has also achieved the elite Chairman's Cabinet as a Top 50 agent in the company, also awarded for production. Given that New York Life has over 12,000 agents, that's a nice feat.

Christie's achievements have been in large part dependent on the needs of her clients as well. Although she focuses on those needing retirement income, Christie has been able to assist clients in many other areas, such as the need for long-term care insurance.

I have known Christie for almost 15 years. In that time, I have watched her bloom into a top producing female advisor. When I worked there as a company officer, she would attend all of my meetings, sitting in the front row, using her tape recorder so that she could listen to the concepts over and over later while driving to appointments. As a seminar speaker for her on a number of occasions, I recognize the great people she has turned into clients over the years. Most of all, she has been able to help so many of those clients retire comfortably.

Advice from Christie

For those who are considering working in the arena of lifetime income or solutions, Christie has several pieces of advice. First, stick with it. Although she had her struggles in the beginning, she now realizes that this business doesn't have to be hard.

A big part of attaining success in the financial field overall is to determine what it is that you are passionate about. Be informed and listen closely to your clients in order to understand what they really need.

In addition, successful agents need to find a way to stand out while at the same time being genuine. People will naturally gravitate to those who they feel are authentic. A big part of this is having a story to tell. This will help you to know what works in real situations.

It goes without saying that the insurance business can offer a great opportunity for female agents. Christie often shares her story of success with other women who are considering a career change into the insurance field. She tells them that with this career, they can truly control their lives, run a profitable and rewarding business, and still have time to spend with their family. On top of that, because women can be such good and caring listeners, Christie feels that females are naturals for helping people plan to achieve their financial goals and dreams.

One way that Christie has opted to take even more control of her time is by hiring two assistants. After several years of attempting to do everything herself, she found that she was burning the candle at both ends, meeting with clients during the day and wading through piles of paperwork at night.

Now, running offices in two locations, Christie is able to manage her time much better with the help of Jann and Connie. They take care of all administrative details, allowing Christie to devote her entire time to meeting with clients. Christie readily admits that she could not run her business without them.

To be successful in this business, you have to believe that you can truly help everyone whom you meet. In one respect, many individuals—especially the soon-to-be-retiring baby boomers—are overwhelmed with the financial information that is available to them. They are seeking relationships with a professional whom they can trust. In return, these agents can really educate and help them plan to live comfortably in their retirement years.

Knowing now that it simply took a change in attitude in order to turn her career from struggling to success, Christie firmly believes that the only thing stopping many professionals in the financial field is themselves. With the right frame of mind and motivation, coupled with a genuine work ethic, you can truly be unstoppable.

**For additional information on Christie,
visit www.christiemueller.com**

This section represents a general overview of how Christie Mueller started her career in financial services and how certain principals, training, and experience have helped her to be effective in the area of retirement income planning. Neither Christie Mueller, nor Christie Mueller and Associates is affiliated with the author, Tom Hegna. Nothing in this chapter is to be considered and offer of any specific product or service, nor is it intended to provide any specific tax advice. Readers are advised to consult a professional focused in the areas discussed to help them address their specific situation.

Key Points

- Have a story and then relate it to your clients. It will be easier for them to see how the products can work for them if they have a frame of reference.

- Don't close your mind without getting well-informed.

- Persevere—especially in times of struggle.

- Helping clients obtain peace of mind can be priceless.

- Lifetime income annuities not only provide incoming cash flow but can also help enhance the quality of a client's life.

- Don't automatically rule out anyone for lifetime income, regardless of how much money they already have.

- Converting assets to income can also help older clients to be less appealing as targets of scams.

- Your achievements are based in large part on helping your clients meet their goals and objectives.

- Determine what you are passionate about and find a way to stand out.

- The insurance business can provide many opportunities for women.

- The only thing that can really stop you is yourself.

Joseph W. Jordan
(Photo © Natalie Brasington)

Chapter 13: Significantly Improving Clients' Lives

"Living a life of significance begins with impact that you can have on the lives of your clients."

Joseph W. Jordan
Independent Consultant

People don't really buy products—they buy people. They choose people whom they feel they can trust and people who are helping them accomplish their emotional goals. While many agents fall into the trap of touting statistics and showing an endless array of charts and graphs, the real reason that people buy—even if the products make good financial sense in and of themselves—is that they connect with the agent on a deeper level.

Joseph W. Jordan, independent consultant, author, and speaker, stresses these concepts to the financial services representatives with whom he works. A former Senior Vice President of MetLife, Joe is an industry-renowned thought leader in the areas of behavioral finance, client-centric tools, ethical selling, and client advocacy. He helps financial professionals around the world recognize and celebrate the intrinsic value that they deliver to their clients.

Anyone who sells financial protection products or works in a financial planning organization may already be familiar with Joe Jordan. Joe speaks to audiences of financial services professionals worldwide, prompting them to connect with clients and prospects in a new way—primarily by using a new behavioral finance theory that highlights just how important one's emotions are in making financial decisions.

> Very early, Joe learned that financial planning is much less about numbers on a graph and more about the impact that it has on peoples' lives. Growing up in New York City, Joe learned firsthand the importance of planning—and sticking with the plan. His father passed away in an auto accident at an early age, after just having canceled a very sizable life insurance policy. "My family's life would have been a lot different if he hadn't canceled it," Joe realized. For this reason, he chose to focus his abilities on helping others avoid similar situations and to teach other agents that clients are, first and foremost, people with real lives.

With over 36 years of experience—from life insurance sales to Wall Street to MetLife—Joe offers compelling insights into the financial services industry, illustrating the concept of managing behavior and demonstrating how to emotionally engage customers.

Joe is known for his passion in helping others to discover the significant and lasting impact that financial professionals have on the lives of others. He has spoken on the main platform at the Million Dollar Round Table (MDRT) annual meeting, as well as other MDRT events around the world in such countries as Thailand, Ireland, Greece, Hong Kong, and Australia, among many others. He was the keynote speaker at the Life Insurance and Market Research Association (LIMRA) Distribution conference in Hong Kong in 2012 and was the chairman of the Personal Finance Society's conference in the United Kingdom, which is one of the largest Independent Financial Adviser's conventions in the UK.

Arguably one of the world's greatest and most well-known annuity and insurance trainers—due in large part to his unique approach—Joe Jordan helps agents become more successful by first getting them to understand that they aren't really "selling" anything.

Joe Jordan started his career with Home Life in 1974, where he was named "Rookie of the Year" and a member of the Million Dollar Round Table. Joe ran insurance sales at Paine Webber from 1981 to 1988 until he joined MetLife to manage annuity sales, product development, and, later, life insurance. He also started fee-based financial planning at MetLife and was ultimately responsible for MetLife's Behavioral Finance Strategies.

Since 2010, Joe has been selected as one of the Top 50 Irish Americans on Wall Street for 3 years in a row. Currently, he lives in Manhattan with his wife; together, they have two children. He is a member of the Fordham University Football Hall of Fame, and he also played rugby for over 30 years with the New York Athletic Club. He is truly a team player, and his experience on the field has ingrained in him the knowledge of connecting with others to be successful together.

Joe focuses on the concept that people are not motivated by facts. Rather, they act on their emotions. In most instances, individuals don't always do what they know they should do; instead they do what they feel is right.

In this vein, Joe stresses that advisors must stop focusing on product performance and start concentrating on their clients' goals. The only way to learn about these goals is by truly listening to the clients, not by showing them spreadsheets. Therefore, when working with financial professionals, Joe emphasizes that the first rule is not to sell, but rather to establish relationships. Joe is fond of quoting Phil Harriman, former president of the Million Dollar Round Table and also a personal friend of mine, who says, "Clients take action for reasons they come to on their own." The role of the financial advisor is to find those reasons, those dreams, those goals—and only then can a plan be constructed around those desires. By helping clients feel safe, comfortable, and well-informed, the rest will fall into place.

Example

If, for example, a couple is purchasing a home, it is likely that they will also need a mortgage in order to finance the purchase. Rather than viewing this as a financial issue, Joe sees it as an emotional one. Getting those funds to purchase the home will not just allow the couple to move in to a physical "brick and mortar" structure, it makes it possible for them to create memories and experiences.

Joe asserts that it requires real, tangible, and emotional goals in order to achieve successful long-term investing. Otherwise, clients tend to rely more on market factors and they may, in fact, attach the success of their investing on market performance alone. This is where advisors must understand that they have to first determine a client's financial goals before any type of product or strategy can be used in moving that client toward those goals. [94]

Understanding people's goals and emotions is good business. Dealing with people's emotions not only gets people to act, but reinforces the satisfaction and fulfillment of the financial professional. In order to create an emotional connection with clients, it is important to first have a true belief in how you are helping them. If agents don't believe in what they do, their clients will subsequently struggle to maintain faith in them and their abilities.

Defining purpose is crucial for both an agent's and a company's overall success. "If someone is disrespectful of you or treats you like a used car salesman, do you know what you tell them? You tell them this: What I do for a living is I protect the innocent when someone dies prematurely. I provide a worry-free retirement that people can't outlive. I protect their assets when they get sick. I provide a legacy when they die because I live a life of significance." [95]

In reality, the financial services business is built on a foundation of trust—trust by the clients in the agents who serve them. Agents can essentially build this trust by having a firm belief in what it is

94 Joseph W. Jordan, Living a Life of Significance, Second Edition (Boston: Acanthus Publishing, 2013).
95 Ibid.

that they are offering, along with a belief in how their products and services will truly bring clients closer to their financial goals. Without this trust, it really doesn't matter how much product or industry knowledge an agent has, they simply won't succeed. At best, it will be a constant struggle.

One of the surest ways to combat the negative feelings from rejection and to preserve a good, strong, and positive belief in yourself is to know ahead of time what you will say and how you will say it. Think about it in terms of "scripting" the conversation. When agents prepare what they will say, they project more credibility and the client is more trusting, leading to a much deeper client-advisor relationship. [96]

This preparation is evident both with agents in the field and those in the home office. In my experience, many home office people fail to realize how important confidence and language really is to their new agents. When I was a new agent for MetLife, Joe mesmerized me at many a meeting. More than that, he gave me the words to say to my clients and the confidence that what I was doing was important. In my first book, *Paychecks and Playchecks*, I acknowledged Joe as one of the three most important people in my life.

I still remember how he explained "The Equalizer," a feature on the MetLife variable annuity that would rebalance an account that was half S&P 500, half fixed. He used two pitchers of different-colored liquids and would show how you would "automatically buy low and sell high." He would ask, "How do you make money in the market?" And the audience would reply in unison, "Buy low and sell high." This wasn't rocket science—he just made simple concepts come to life.

I also remember at a council meeting, Joe was dressed as a surgeon. He and a partner were "operating" on another executive, who was laid out on an operation table. They said that he had a tax problem and needed some type of tax "bypass"—more formally called, a tax deferral. On all of our seats were "prescription pads" prescribing Tax Deferral to our clients. I learned from Joe that speaking at the highest level was not just about facts or numbers— it was really about stories with just enough showmanship thrown in for good measure.

When Joe heard the lesson told by Dick Austin about the "drive in the desert" horror story (Chapter 9), Joe knew that he was in the right market niche. The story profoundly illustrated the importance of how people feel about and how they react to the possibility of not having enough income to last throughout their lives.

Listening to this story suddenly "put a human face" on the possibility of running out of money—and how terrible it would feel. It was done without the use of statistics, numbers, graphs, charts, or a fancy presentation. It simply demonstrated the true angst and anguish of the actual running out of money, along with the long-lasting fear and anticipation of doing so. Such a feeling can literally last for years. Due in large part to the story of the desert, Joe moved into the behavioral finance arena, so that he could alleviate the feeling of impending disaster when "driving in the desert."

Throughout his years in the insurance business, Joe came to the realization that people use both sides of their brain to make financial decisions. While the right side of the brain deals with emotions, connections, and beliefs, the left side justifies choices based on facts, figures, and analysis. Because of this, people don't always seem to behave in a rational or predictable manner when making even the most important of decisions.

This, Joe says, is where behavioral finance comes into play. This particular area of economics deals with how the choices people make are really influenced by factors that span far beyond just the logic of the situation.

It's important to always keep in mind that financial services are in many ways much more of an emotional sale than an analytical one. This is especially true when working with protection products like life insurance and annuities.

So how can agents prepare themselves to work more on an emotional level with clients? One of the best ways to do so is to rethink how the concept of insurance is discussed. For example, rather than focusing on the "face amount" of a life insurance policy, view it as an income replacement for the loved ones who would be affected if the policy holder were no longer there.

There are also certain types of questions that can be asked of clients to uncover their needs. Oftentimes, by simply asking the right questions, agents may even find that clients create their own solutions in answering the question.

The questions don't need to be complicated, either—sometimes just a yes/no or an agree/disagree format will do. Joe gave the following examples for a 2010 article in *Agent's Sales Journal*, which are designed around behavioral finance concepts:

- "I prefer a predictable retirement income check each month, like a regular paycheck, in exchange for giving up some of my ability to take more income when I may need it."

- "It's important for me to have a large portion of my retirement savings available at all times for things like unexpected home repairs or family emergencies, even though that may mean less income is available throughout my retirement years."

- "Having the flexibility to use my assets to generate the income I want today is important to me, even if it means I may run out of assets and have no income later on."

- "I would be comfortable giving up access to my retirement savings in order to receive the most income possible." [97]

By asking these emotional types of questions, an analytical approach can become much more balanced in terms of helping clients to actually see themselves earning income and managing their assets during retirement. They are not designed to educate clients; instead, they should help an advisor discover how a client feels about those decisions.

Through framing, the advisor can see what a client feels about a certain financial matter. For example, the first bullet frames the idea

---

[97] Joseph W. Jordan, "How to Ask the Right Questions to Sell More Annuities,"Agent's Sales Journal in LifeHealth-Pro, November 8, 2010, http://www.lifehealthpro.com/2010/11/08/how-to-ask-the-right-questions-to-sell-more-annuit.

of income—and most clients would answer "True." From there, the advisor can explain to their client how that feeling translates into a financial plan. But the last bullet is actually the same question framed as an investment; yet most people would answer "False." The trade off to saying true to the first bullet is having to say true to the last. These questions are designed to help clients see the "tyranny of the decision."

It's a process that combines fact with feeling. Through the discussions an advisor has with clients, he can help clients take action for reasons they come to on their own, as Phil Harriman likes to say.

Clients don't want a product; they want a process. "The problem is not the problem; the problem is, they don't know how to think about the problem," Joe explains. They want a process that helps them see how they feel and then create their own solution.

Real success in the financial services world isn't necessarily measured by the size of the commission check—or at least, it shouldn't be. The real success stories come from those agents who are able to take clients' problems and solve them, not just sell them a product.

Case Study

Joe Jordan's book *Living a Life of Significance* chronicles Joe's life experiences and his passion for helping others to achieve financial security. He highlights several agents' stories where life insurance made a real difference in someone's life—and without it, struggle would have surely ensued. Here is one of the stories from a longtime agent and financial planner:

My client, Sally, came to me to discuss insurance for her small business. As we talked about the right policy for her business, I inquired about her personal retirement plan, of which she apparently had none. "You really should pressure your employer to offer that benefit," I laughed.

Taking a more serious note, I outlined the importance for someone at her young age to build a retirement plan so that she could begin to accumulate savings to use in her old age and with which to create a legacy for her family.

Sally understood the importance of taking these actions and reserved money for retirement. She also decided to opt into a universal life plan with her mother as the recipient so that, if anything happened her, her mother was not left in utter financial chaos. When her dad passed away, he had not been as proactive with life insurance and her mother had to struggle over the consequences.

After a few years, Sally realized that she could manage to expand her shop by purchasing her aunt's. She had agreed on an installment plan with her so that she could guarantee it was paid for no matter what. I wrote up a policy with an annual convertible term that Wednesday.

On Saturday, Sally died in an auto accident. Her mother inherited Sally's life insurance funds, which she would use to retire comfortably. The money reserved to cover her installment plan was given to her aunt, who was in failing health herself.

Sally's sister was then given responsiblity of both businesses—debt free because of Sally's careful planning. When Sally's sister married and was having difficulty getting pregnant, the absence of financial stress from the two inherited businesses meant that she and her husband could afford to adopt a child. When they realized that they would be adding a beautiful baby girl to their family, it seemed obvious that she be named Sally after the loving and thoughtful aunt whom she would never meet.

Years later when Sally's sister came to thank me and tell me this story, it became clear that the planning I had advised Sally to make had created a beautiful legacy for her family. Instead of simply leaving money, Sally had left behind love letters. The letter to her mother said, "Mom, you deserve a comfortable retirement and I am thankful to be able to give that gift to you." To her aunt--"I gave you my word to pay you for your business and I will live up to my commitment to you." Her sister--"These businesses I trust to you but without financial worry because I appreciate what you are doing for me." And the letter she never knew she was writing was to her namesake--"While we will never know each other, I am honored to live on through you." I felt that my work had become so paramount to the future of this family.[98]

Through the story of Sally, Joe is able to highlight just how much more emotional a client-advisor relationship is. When an agent connects with a client on an emotional level, they become an advocate. They essentially bring the humanity back in to a sales process that has become far too dependent upon fancy graphs and complicated numerical projections.

Equally as important, though, is when representatives bring passion and motivation to themselves, as well as to their clients. When they accomplish this, the agent wholeheartedly believes that they are truly doing one of the most important jobs in the world.

As an agent, always remember that you live a life of significance. By approaching a client with their best interests at heart, you are always doing the right thing. They feel it and respond. You will not only earn that client's business, but you will feel terrific about the impact that you are making on their lives.

98 Joseph W. Jordan, *Living a Life of Significance.*

Advice from Joe

Joe offers several tips for helping financial professionals put behavioral science concepts into practice. He helps them bring more value to the table and build their businesses based on trust and relationships rather than products and performance.

First, while it is never easy to turn business away, there are times when agents should consider passing on working with a particular client. This is especially the case with clients who only care about top performance of products. Typically, these clients will nearly always flee at the first sign of volatility anyway and will never stay with one financial advisor for very long.

Next, agents should realize that people are paying for you—and not your products. Price is typically only an issue in the absence of value. Keeping this in mind will also help an agent stay motivated in the face of both objection and rejection.

Third, there are three primary types of people in the world: those who will listen to your advice, those who won't listen to your advice, and those who have not yet heard your advice. Keep the first, lose the second, and talk with the third to make them into the first.

And last, but certainly not by any means the least, everybody will die. Therefore, wouldn't it be nice to make a difference in the people's lives who are affected? By letting clients know that you are there to help them, your business will grow exponentially.

For more information about Joe Jordan and his *Living a Life of Significance*, visit: www.josephjordan.com

Key Points

- People don't buy products, they buy people.

- Stop focusing on product performance and start focusing on clients' goals.

- In order to create an emotional connection with clients, it is important to first have a true belief in how you are helping them.

- People use both sides of their brains to make decisions—using emotion and facts.

- Rather than focusing on the face amount of a life insurance policy, it should instead be looked at as income replacement for the family and loved ones who would be affected if the policyholder were no longer there.

- Financial professionals need to realize that success is not about you—and that true significance is much more about the impact that you have on the lives of others.

- True value shouldn't be measured by the amount of money that you make, but rather by the size of the problem you can solve.

Chapter 14:
How Much of a Difference Can You Make?

"If money wasn't an issue in your life, what would you do?"

Rao K. Garuda, CLU®, ChFC®
Associated Concepts Agency, Inc. / First Financial Resources, LLC

Rao K. Garuda
(Photo courtesy of Rao Garuda)

The biggest fear today in retirees' and pre-retirees' minds is of running out of money. But lifetime income annuities can alleviate this fear. They reduce the constant worry and stress about life's everyday and ongoing expenses. Just the knowledge of having a guaranteed lifetime income can improve countless other aspects of their lives. Clients can then focus their time and energy on actually living their life.

Rao K. Garuda, CLU®, ChFC®, president and CEO of Associated Concepts Agency, understands this paralyzing fear. Since he founded his financial services advisory company in 1978, he seeks to assuage this worry. He asks many of his clients, "If you're constantly worried about the market, what does it do to the quality of your life?"

To maintain a better quality of life for their clients, his company focuses on the ways and means to reduce the tension of taxes and other pressing financial issues. They accomplish this by setting up predictable, safe, and consistent income streams that will last throughout their clients' retirement years—regardless of how long that may be.

> Rao Garuda understands firsthand the fear of running out of money and the stress it can cause. When he arrived at JFK Airport from India nearly five decades ago, he only had $7 in his pocket and a dream of making a difference. Imagine—arriving in a foreign country, speaking a different language, and barely having enough money for dinner. As his father could only lend enough money for a one-way airline ticket, he advised his son to be a success—not much different than Cortez burning all his ships when he attacked Mexico so that his soldiers had to fight to win, since there was no retreat.

> Rao came to America as a teaching assistant to pursue graduate work in structural engineering, after graduating with the highest GPA from his engineering college in India and being offered a full scholarship to the University of Colorado. He attended graduate school at the University of Colorado and Colorado State University. Rao was offered his first job in Cleveland, Ohio. Four years later, after going back to India to marry, he and his bride made Cleveland their permanent home.

Despite this unlikely start, Rao entered the financial services business in the 1970s. He initially invested in limited partnerships, real estate, and the stock market. For roughly the first 10 years of his career, Rao and his clients ended up losing money using these strategies. Rao says part of the reason for this was that "emotion always trumps logic." Knowing that he needed a change, Rao searched for more of a system in which to better help his clients and grow his business.

> Before turning to finance, Rao had begun his working career as an engineer. His 1976 annual income of $140,000 put him in the 70% marginal tax bracket and he found himself having to borrow funds from his physician wife to pay his income taxes. He took a hard look at how he could help himself and others to

lower their tax obligations and entered into the financial services business. His primary niche has always been taxes—even today, this is how he brings many new clients through his door.

With his deep knowledge of the US tax system, Rao is able to reduce his clients' taxes by setting up various strategies for lessening both income and estate taxes for his clients. In doing so, he enables his clients to retain more funds to put toward income generation— so it's really a win-win all around.

In Rao's business, he and his team focus on providing clients with the income they need to cover both basic and discretionary expenses in retirement. This can be done by using qualified money from 401(k) plans, for example, as well as from other non-qualified funds.

On top of working with his own clients, Rao also spends time teaching and mentoring other financial services professionals so that they too can pass along lifetime income and tax reduction strategies to their customers as well.[99]

Case Study

Rao met with a couple—both doctors—who each held $2.5 million in IRA accounts. In going over their investments, Rao discovered that 100% of the couple's money was invested in the stock market.

He could see that the couple was uneasy about the volatility of the market but, at the same time, wanted to earn a nice return. Rao then asked the couple, "If I could give you the same paycheck that you're getting now—regardless of how long you live—and also remove the market concern, as well as allow you to transfer assets to your heirs, would we have something to talk about?"

The wife, an established psychiatrist, responded to Rao's easy-to-understand explanation of guaranteed lifetime

99 Rao K. Garuda, "About," Rao K Garuda: Twenty-first Century Advisor, 2012, http://www.raokgaruda.com/about/.

income simply with, "How come nobody else talks about it like that?" At that, Rao earned a $5 million lifetime income annuity case and life insurance as well, since the cash flow was much more than required to maintain their lifestyle.

Oftentimes, Rao leads a meeting by stating to his prospects, "I happen to believe that you're paying too much in taxes." Because he tends to focus on high-net-worth individuals, specifically those in the medical field, they jump at his help.

Rao's Favorite Statements for Doctors:

• Would you like an MRI of your portfolio? We see danger before danger sees you.

• Taxes are just like cancer.

• When is the last time you had a full executive check up with a "financial stress test?"

• A "cashectomy" will be performed on your qualified plan assets. We like to show you better choices.

• You have too much L.D.L. [the lousy cholesterol] in your stock portfolio; we would like to balance it.

Over time, Rao has fine-tuned his business system by essentially addressing three key areas with his clients. He first creates a guaranteed stream of income for clients, then focuses on tax-sensitive issues, which include the cutting of taxes on that created income. Last, using the creditor protection feature of annuities, Rao helps clients protect themselves from lawsuits, liens, and judgments.[100]

Rao intended to go to law school after his Master's degree, but—due to his interest in taxes—the dean of the law school convinced Rao to instead pursue his degree in business. At his suggestion, Rao completed a two-

---

100 This protection varies by state.

year paralegal program and graduated from the Ohio Paralegal Institute. It was there that one of his income tax law professors introduced him to the insurance and financial services industry.

Soon afterward, Rao began working for National Life. Within two short years, he had become an independent advisor—and a very successful one at that! In Rao's first year, he earned over $200,000 in income and was soon thereafter earning seven figures per year—a far cry from the $140,000 that he was previously earning as a vice president in the engineering field. He focused on how to qualify for the prestigious Million Dollar Round Table's Top of the Table, the highest honor any agent can aspire to achieve. He realized the secret is "collaboration, not competition."

Although it's hard to top putting together 26 pension plans for clients in his first year as a financial planner, Rao has consistently done well ever since, keeping him in the coveted Top of the Table of the Million Dollar Roundtable for 21 consecutive years! Today, Rao is a member and director of Forum 400 and spends his time conducting seminars on asset protection, tax reduction, retirement income, charitable giving, and estate planning issues.

In a nutshell, Rao helps his clients set up income streams and then shows them how to save taxes on that income. In order to create guaranteed paychecks, he works with clients in setting up lifetime income annuities. Since their income needs are taken care of for the long term with an annuity, his clients can do more of what they want with their lives.

Case Study

Rao was meeting with a 65-year-old doctor from India. He asked the prospect his standard question: "If money wasn't an issue in your life, what would you do?" The doctor told Rao that he had always wanted to accomplish one thing, but that nobody could show him how. His dream was to be able to send 10 students to medical school in India each year for the rest of his life.

Rao concluded that the doctor could not only accomplish his dream by using a lifetime income annuity, but that he could do so by simply moving $100,000 to a 501c3 and using the income from that.

When the time came for the client to write the $100,000 check, his hands started shaking and he began to cry. Hugging Rao, the grateful client told him, "You have no idea what you have done for me." Helping clients achieve their dreams is what makes Rao's job so rewarding.

Rao knows that there simply aren't many financial advisors who can do what he does: show clients how to get a guaranteed paycheck for life. Clients often tell Rao that no other advisor has been able to show them exactly how to accomplish their financial goals like he has. In the 15-plus years that Rao has been using lifetime income annuities, he has helped countless clients through annuities.

Like me, Rao is an ongoing student of financial planning techniques, especially as it relates to income annuities. He is constantly updating his knowledge by taking courses, attending workshops, and reading published materials from a number of different sources.

One piece in particular, a Financial Research Corporation white paper titled "Income Annuities Improve Portfolio Outcomes in Retirement," argues that other products simply can't compete with features of the income annuity, including high cash flow, no correlation to market volatility, and retirement alpha in the form of mortality credits. It continues, "There is literally no other vehicle in the marketplace that can convert assets into income as efficiently as the income annuity."[101] Using these materials, Rao is able to gain additional trust from his clients when putting together retirement income plans.

---

101 Scott DeMonte and Lawrence Petrone, "Income Annuities Improve Portfolio Outcomes in Retirement," Financial Research Corporation, 2012.

Throughout his career, Rao has learned a lot of his strategies by using his own money. "You have to eat your own cooking," he says. Not only does Rao already own lifetime income annuities for himself and his wife, but he recently advised his 38-year-old son on how to plan for retirement, so he could avoid working in his retirement years—a clear indication that even the younger generation is beginning to worry about having an income that they can count on for the future.

Like so many of his clients, Rao's success has allowed both him and his family to live the life of their dreams. His wife enjoyed a successful career as an anesthesiologist until a heart surgery made them realize how unnecessary the undue stress was putting on her life.

He and his wife have two sons who are both highly accomplished in their own fields—one as a physician and the other as a managing director for a major financial services company. Like his father, the son following in his father's footsteps learned the power of hard work, graduating second out of 1,600 in his class at Harvard. Rao, with four brothers and a sister, states that his own father was quite strict and that he would not tolerate getting a bad grade in school. Rao appreciated such training and passed it on to his own children as well.

Even though Rao knows that he could have retired a wealthy man many years ago, he continues to meet with clients for the purpose of sharing how they can create a guaranteed lifetime income and reduce their tax burden.

Today, Rao conducts seminars with groups of 50 to 100 doctors, with a primary focus on specialists. He knows that these individuals typically earn higher incomes and therefore have a greater need to reduce their amount of income taxation. Rao also sends out direct mail to lists of high-net-worth individuals.

Case Study

Rao had a couple attend three of his dinner seminars before finally making an appointment to see him. The couple apologized for eating so many "free dinners," but explained that they were having trouble understanding the concept of the guaranteed paycheck for life.

Upon setting up a meeting with them, Rao asked if they would bring in their current financial statements. When the couple arrived with a large Samsonite suitcase loaded with statements—some 200 and 300 pages long—Rao knew that changes would need to be made.

All told, the couple had roughly $5.5 million in investable assets. Once the amount had been totaled, the husband asked Rao to "go do his thing." When Rao asked, "What exactly is my thing?" the client said, "You know—that guaranteed paycheck thing."

The clients wanted to put all of their money into an annuity that had a guaranteed lifetime income benefit rider. When Rao told them that his broker-dealer would not allow all of a client's assets to be put into one type of product, the client insisted further—finally asking to speak to the broker-dealer himself.

When Rao got the chief of compliance on the phone, even he could not deter the clients from their decision. When the compliance officer stated that the clients would need to keep at least some of their assets liquid, the clients responded that they could take 10% of their funds out of the annuity without a surrender charge—and that would be in excess of $500,000. Since they only needed $50,000 to live on, liquidity would not be a problem.

When the clients agreed to put their wishes in writing, the broker-dealer arranged to let the case go through, providing Rao with a $5 million annuity case. To make this story even better is the fact that this occurred in 2005—three years before the market crash.

Rao recently spoke with these clients to verify that all of their money was still safe. The clients revealed that several of their other advisors had told them at the time that they were

> foolish for going through with the annuity transaction. Today, however, with 100% of their money still safe, the clients told Rao that they feel pretty good about being "foolish."

Like that Samsonite bag full of papers, Rao has had numerous cases where he has been able to make the complicated easy. Once he explains how guaranteed lifetime income works, he rarely gets objections. This is in large part due to the fact that this strategy answers clients' concerns while at the same time not forcing them to give up return. It is this simple way of showing clients how they will benefit, both in the short and the long term, that moves them forward.

Due to his clear focus on what he offers and whom he offers it to, Rao has also had great success with referrals. In one case, he was introduced to 22 people from just one of his satisfied clients!

I first met Rao Garuda when I spoke at a Top of the Table meeting for the Million Dollar Round Table back in 2009. Rao came up to me to discuss my Paychecks and Playchecks presentation and it was immediately apparent that Rao was a student of our business. Since that time, I have seen Rao over and over again at key industry meetings. Sometimes I have seen him 3 times in a 2-week period. Although Rao possesses several degrees, he continues to attend numerous educational seminars every year. Rao quotes something that his own father told him many years ago—"The greatest gift I can give you is the gift of education."

Rao has truly taken that to heart, keeping continuous education a lifelong mission. He states that you can never know too much—and, with the constantly changing tax and finance world, there is always something new to learn and master to help your clients. Each year, Rao takes three months to attend seminars and to educate himself. As a firm believer in charitable giving, Rao takes another three months to participate in charitable activities and travel.

Over the years, Rao has realized just how much of a difference that he has made in the lives of his clients. While he is happy to have accomplished that, he has expanded his lifetime goals. Today, Rao says it's not about how much money he makes, but how much of a difference he can make. He is driven by his desire to make $500 million for a variety of different charities that are close to his heart. Personally, Rao and his wife have already contributed over $1 million to various charities. Today, with no worries about running out of money, he can focus on others.

He sums up his current future by stating, "With your needs taken care of and no more financial struggle, there really isn't much pressure. At this point, you can truly do what is best for the client, regardless of how much money you will make selling a particular product. And, you can really focus on making a difference." Rao also feels that once the clients are at peace with their income needs, they can focus on what's near and dear to their hearts. "Our goal is to help our clients move from Good to Great to Exceptional. The products we use allow us to do this."

One of Rao's favorite approaches with a successful business owner is saying, "I am told there are two very important days in everybody's life; the first is the day you are born, the second is the day you find out why." Once a client hears this, the conversation changes. It becomes, "How soon can we get started?" The conversation is from the "heart," not the "head." Rao's philosophy of "serve and deserve" can best be summed up by the quotation from Mahatma Gandhi and Sri Sathya Sai Baba, who said, "My life is my message and it's a message of love."

Advice from Rao

To those of you who wish to focus on the retiree and pre-retiree market, Rao has several pieces of advice to help ensure success. They obviously work, as Rao has not only created a highly successful business, he also mentors over 50 agents nationwide.

First, learn all that you possibly can about lifetime income annuities. The best way to do that is by reading *Paychecks and Playchecks*. When reading, don't just gloss over the concepts. Really, truly learn how and why these products can add value. Become so knowledgeable about these vehicles that you are considered an expert. Learn key concepts like covering basic expenses with guaranteed lifetime income then optimizing the rest of the portfolio to reduce taxes and protect against inflation. Truly understand mortality credits and why they are so powerful when recommending both life insurance and lifetime income annuities.

Next, learn all that you possibly can about your clients' needs. Remember to listen to WIIFM radio—"What's In It For Me." When you do so, you will truly hear your client's goals and aspirations. It is likely that they will have income needs; however, their goals and dreams will all be unique.

Once their everyday living expenses are taken care of with a guaranteed paycheck for life, you can then work with clients on their more discretionary income needs. This will also gain you their trust—ultimately resulting in the accumulation of more assets under management.

Remember, though, it isn't so much about numbers, percentages, payouts, or illustrations. It is a very simple strategy—make a difference in your clients' lives. If you can provide them with a way to receive a guaranteed income for life, you will have addressed their biggest fear.

**For additional information about Rao K. Garuda,
visit: http://aca-incorp.com**

Key Points

• Today, the biggest fear in retirees' and pre-retirees' lives is of running out of money.

• Once basic income needs are taken care of, people can do what they really want to do with their lives.

• If you can provide clients with a way to receive a guaranteed income for life, you will have addressed their biggest fear.

• Using a fine-tuned system can help you to focus on the areas where you can help clients the most.

• Lifetime income annuities offer features that other products simply cannot compete with—including high cash flow, no correlation to market volatility, and retirement alpha in the form of mortality credits.

• "You have to eat your own cooking." Practice what you preach.

• The greatest gift you can give is the gift of education, which includes offering clients advice that can help them accomplish their goals and dreams.

• Learn all that you possibly can about annuities— become an expert.

Conclusion

What you uniquely offer to clients is the greatest tool that an advisor can possess. I hope that through the stories of these successful advisors, you have realized what skills and perspective that only you have—this is your strength. Conversely, you should also have realized your weaknesses through the strengths of others. Their advice and example can be the means to go about improving what you lack.

My question now is which chapter affected you the most?

Was it John Schwan's "little blue work card"? Rao Garuda's overwhelmingly appreciative Indian doctor? Curtis Cloke's REFIREMENT?

Did you connect with Joe Jordan's assertion that your value is not measured by how much money you make, but by the size of the problem you can solve? Bob Hartman's distinction between "want" and "need"? John Olsen's view that lifetime income annuities are really risk transfer devices?

Or did Michael Kitces' coolness toward lifetime income annuities strike a chord?

What did you think about Dick Austin's "extended unemployment"?

Christie Mueller's drastic change in attitude that turned her career from struggling to success? Dave Christy's decision to hire where his weaknesses are?

Were you inspired by John Curry's Secure Retirement Method? Briggs Matsko's Retirement Security Centers? John Homer's Guaranteed Income Plan? Or Michael Gordon's sustainable income?

For me, there were several that really hit home.

The panic of Dick Austin's drive in the desert where the family knows that they are going to run out of gas. Those feelings get me every time—I have even incorporated that story into my main platform presentations.

The passion of Michael Kitces, who argues against my core beliefs but does it so well.[104]

The inspiration of Rao Garuda going from $7 in his pocket to a multi-multi-millionaire whose goals have now turned to charity. The insightfulness of Dave Christy who believes that lifetime income is a strong client retention tool.

The acumen of Dr. DIA himself, Curtis Cloke. John Olsen's deep understanding of risk. The expertness of Briggs Matsko, the sophisticated simplicity of John Curry, the drive and thoughtfulness of Christie Mueller. The peace of mind and sophisticated research offered by Michael Gordon. Bob Hartman's world class service. Or Mr. Inspiration himself—Joe Jordan.

The humble power of John Schwan and the creativity of John Homer.

Each advisor is a master in their own right. Any skill or advice that you can glean from them will make you a better advisor and a better person.

No matter the strengths or weaknesses of any advisor, we must help clients deal with the current low interest rate environment. While many may think that higher rates and inflation are around the corner,

---

[104] Michael recently teamed up with American College Professor Wade Pfau to write a research paper comparing a lifetime income annuity to a more traditional bucket strategy titled "The True Impact of Immediate Annuities on Retirement Sustainability: A Total Wealth Perspective." While I partook in a lively debate with the other Masters in regards to those findings, I find the research more academic than practical. To see for yourself, please visit http://ssrn.com/abstract=2296867.

I am not convinced. The massive government debt at all levels of government that will eventually need to be reduced or deleveraged, combined with the economic consequences of an aging country and the world at large, will place deflationary pressures on our economy for decades! The Federal Reserve's unprecedented rate of printing money would normally be inflationary, maybe even hyperinflationary. But, as I said in Paychecks and Playchecks, these are not normal times.

This low interest rate environment has immediate impacts on your client's insurance and retirement savings.

First of all, I would be so bold as to say that everyone reading this book is currently underinsured for life insurance: In a 1% interest rate environment, it takes $5,000,000 of life insurance to protect every $50,000 of income. How many clients do you have that make $50,000 per year who also have $5,000,000 of life insurance? Not many, I'm assuming.

While some of you may say, "Tom, that is ridiculous," I would respond, how much life insurance would you need to protect $50,000 of income if we were in a 5% interest environment? $1,000,000. I firmly believe that we need to be recommending no less than $1,000,000 for every $50,000 of income.

Let me tell you a true story. I recently met with a 47-year-old widow whose husband had been killed unexpectedly in a car accident. She was a stay-at-home mom with two young girls. After expressing my codolences, I asked her to tell me about her financial situation. She revealed that her husband had a $1,000,000 life insurance policy but she never thought she would ever be a "millionaire." She envisioned a few "wants" to use the money, including the building of "a custom house on a lake."

She was absolutely shocked when I explained to her that, in this low interest rate environment, $1,000,000 would not provide that kind of lifestyle: It would only produce $10,000 of annual income. We could maybe push it to $35,000 but most of the research now says a 4% withdrawal rate may not survive 40 or 50 years. "But," she said, "my husband made $250,000 per year!" How could I tell her that $1,000,000 was nowhere near enough life insurance for someone making $250,000 per year?

I wonder—how many of the advisors reading this book right now are in the exact same situation? We must recommend more life insurance in this low interest rate environment!

The second immediate impact of the low interest rate environment has to do with retirement. Throughout my lifetime, if you saved 10% of your income, invested in a diversified portfolio, and rebalanced regularly, you could count on a great retirement. But no more. Saving 10% a year in this low interest rate environment just won't cut it! We need to get our clients saving 15% and 20%, if possible. It's all about numbers: In a 1% interest rate environment, it takes $5,000,000 to produce $50,000 of income.

I have tried to show you how you can do better than that through the stories in this book. My point is, without pensions and with the Social Security reform that must happen, you will need much more of your own money to retire properly. We must get our clients to save more!

We also must plan for long-term care. In my conversations with each of the Masters, there was near-unanimous agreement that no retirement plan is complete without a plan for long-term care. I would like to reiterate my own thoughts on long-term care insurance. An unplanned long-term care event is the one thing most seniors forget about that could wipe out everything they own. While actual long-term care policies have seen significant rate increases and reduced benefit offerings, these policies are still very important to the retirement planning process.

I encourage you to take a look at the many combo plans that are now available. Life insurance policies that offer long-term care benefits are becoming very popular. They offer the advantage of using a single dollar to protect multiple risks. For example, the cash value in a life insurance policy can provide tax-free income in retirement. But that same dollar could fund a child's education. If you were to die, that dollar would provide many dollars of a tax-free death benefit and, if you were to need long-term care, that very dollar would provide even more dollars to provide you with the care you need! Annuities are now adding long-term care options, which can be especially valuable to those with pre-existing health conditions. A single dollar can provide multiple options.

For the advisors who haven't, I would encourage you to get your CLTC designation and attend any meeting you can find where Harley Gordon is speaking. He is a true expert in the long-term care arena.

Everyone seems to think that retirement is very complicated. What is the market doing? What are the politicians doing? How is my 401(k) doing? What is the Federal Reserve doing? The more I study retirement, the simpler I see it. It is not about the stock or bond market or Washington, DC. Retirement is very much about income—guaranteed lifetime income! In fact, I believe that the ultimate success of your clients' retirement will depend on the answers to two very simple questions:

1. How much guaranteed lifetime income do they have?

2. Have they taken the key retirement risks—market risk, longevity risk, long-term care, inflation—off the table? How you minimize those risks and maximize their guaranteed lifetime income will truly define the success of their retirement plan.

Especially in this market, we need the best advisors to guide the 78 million baby boomers through the "trials" of retirement. Retirement should be the time to do the things that we didn't have time to do during our working years, without worrying about the status of our funds. Always remember, retirement really is about having the necessary income to be able to live the dreams that you've been planning for all along.